CATHOLIC TRADITIONS

— IN —

Cooking

Ann Ball

Our Sunday Visitor Publishing Division
Our Sunday Visitor, Inc.
Huntington, Indiana 46750

Our Sunday Visitor Publishing Division
Our Sunday Visitor, Inc.
200 Noll Plaza
Huntington, Indiana 46750

International Standard Book Number: 0-87973-531-7
Library of Congress Catalog Card Number: 93-83238

Cover design by Monica Watts
Photograph by John Zierten
Illustrations by Rebecca J. Heaston

PRINTED IN THE UNITED STATES OF AMERICA

531

*This book is dedicated to the Holy Family, my Catholic family,
and my own extended family.*

Contents

Abbreviations

c. = cup(s)	oz. = ounce(s)	tbsp. = tablespoon(s)
doz. = dozen	pkg. = package(s)	tsp. = teaspoon(s)
gal. = gallon(s)	pt. = pint(s)	
lb. = pound(s)	qt. = quart(s)	

Introduction

When I told my son I was writing a cookbook, he hooted with laughter. He, his sister, and the AK's[*] have consistently teased me about my cooking.

When Ed first brought his cousin John to the house, he pointed out the kitchen and called it my "laboratory."

Mark, Michael, Jesse, and Warren thought they had me stumped when they demanded blue food. "Blue on the vine but purple on the plate — we bet you can't serve us blue food!" (I did, and we have since eaten blue food more than once around here.)

Jim will never forgive me for serving him squash (which he hates) and calling it butternut (which it was). The dish was so tasty that he ate it all — and then someone had to ruin it by telling him it was squash. I should have told him about the many times I hid the eggplant on the pizza when the kids were little.

As much as I was teased about my cooking, though, their plates were usually empty when the meal was finished. My daughter finally admitted, "Mom, you are really a pretty good cook, except I didn't like the dog cookies." (She came in once when I had created a recipe for treats for the family pooch and tested them before I could warn her they weren't people food.)

I suppose my love of cooking has rubbed off on the kids, for one of my son's favorite assignments has been as a messcook in the coast guard. His sister has turned out to be a pretty good cook herself. Her first request for a care package from home when she went to Korea was for flour tortilla mix and picante sauce so she could prepare the food-from-home for her new friends.

I have always loved to cook. Two people deserve a special tribute for helping me to become the cook I am today: my grandmother, who let me experiment to my heart's content in her kitchen, and my father, who always ate what I cooked, including the mistakes, and acted as if every bite were wonderful.

In putting together this book, I have enjoyed combining two of my hobbies — cooking and history. Just as cooking is a great part of my own family life, it is also a great part of the family life of my

---

[*]Adopted kids — former students and others who hang around here a lot.

church. Throughout the ages, families drew together for meals and celebrations. What better way to celebrate God's bounty than with tasty foods and family conviviality?

When I first mentioned making a Catholic cookbook, Michael asked, "What makes food Catholic?" I lightly replied that it was food cooked for the church's feasts, or in honor of one of the saints. He snapped back, "Oh, I get it. Well, would you like my recipe for Untidy St. Joseph?" I must have looked a little puzzled because he had to explained, "You know, Sloppy Joe!"

I tried to expand by saying that I would be researching and writing about foods that were traditionally eaten by Catholics through the years. So Jesse joined in the conversation to remind me to include recipes for Blue Food dishes since we were all Catholic and traditionally have eaten this through the years.

Further discussion ensued, and I realized that the project was not going to be quite as simple as it had at first seemed. If I asked for recipes and traditions from Michael's family, I would get Italian customs and foods. If Jesse's family contributed, the food and customs would be Hispanic. And could I include the English-heritage dishes I loved as a child? I only became a Catholic as an adult, but wasn't my Protestant plum pudding the same as that used in pre-Reformation Catholic England?

From the time my children were small I have tried to impress on them the beauty and the diversity of God's people. We collected dolls and coins to help point out the differences and the similarities of all races and cultures. What better way to celebrate than to sample the traditional foods of our brothers in Christ?

Sample is the operative word. In a single book, I could never hope to collect more than a tiny sample of traditional feast-day recipes from the various countries. Thus I have included a bibliography, in hopes that the serious reader who wants to try more of the dishes mentioned in the text will have sources for those mentioned.

The recipes in this book have come from many places. Some were garnered from friends, some from old recipe books. Many were sent to me by members of parishes across the United States and Canada, and some came direct from Catholics in Europe, Asia, and Africa. I am particularly indebted to the bishops of the Eastern rites who sent me information about traditional celebrations in their rites. Too often we in the Western or Latin rite overlook the beauty of the rich heritage claimed by our Eastern brothers in Christ.

I have adapted many of the recipes for the modern kitchen and the modern cook. Today's woman has many demands on her time. Still, she should be able to prepare festive foods for her family. Some recipes do take time to prepare. Some are well worth the time and effort expended.

Another adaptation I have made to many of the recipes is in the matter of spices and ingredients. Although I live in a large multi-national community, many ingredients in the foods native to other countries are hard to find here and completely unavailable in other areas of the country. I have attempted to include only items which might be readily available, and have added a source list in the appendix where certain spices and other ingredients may be mail-ordered.

I strongly believe that it is important to pass tradition and heritage to one's children. For this very reason I baked bread, canned tomatoes, and made jelly with my children. Today we buy these items at the grocery store and do not make them at home on a regular basis. My children, however, understand the specialness of the homemade products. Too, they can feel a closeness to their ancestors who had no handy supermarket just down the street. If I have done nothing better, I am proud of this small bit of knowledge I have passed on to them.

One day when we were making bread, a friend of my son's dropped by. He asked what we were doing. On being told we were baking bread, he refused to believe that it could be made at home! He extended his visit until the bread was done to see if we were "fooling" him. I found this sad as well as funny.

Just as the making of wild plum, crabapple, or mayhaw jelly is a part of my children's East Texas heritage, so too are the traditional foods for the feasts of the Church a part of their Catholic heritage. The taste of mince pie may be the same for believer and non-believer, but it receives its Catholic flavor when we recall that the spices are symbolic of the gifts of the Magi — and that it was originally baked in a shape to recall the manger of Our Lord.

Some of the recipes are ancient, and most of them are very old. That means, of course, that they employ older, traditional cooking methods. In today's society, the need for "quick" cooking has given rise to many shortcuts via microwave and food processor. A seasoned cook will adapt or look on the methods as an adventure.

This is a book to read as well as a book to cook with. It makes no claim to being a complete compendium of Catholic traditional foods. Instead, it sets out patterns and traditions in Catholic cooking in hopes that each cook who reads and uses this book will continue the pattern and pass forward the traditions.

The Christmas Season

Advent

Advent is a moveable observance, beginning on the Sunday closest to the last day in November. This is the celebration that begins the liturgical year — the season that precedes and prepares the way for Christmas. As a preparatory season, Advent started in Rome during the sixth century with a joyful character. Later, the Frankish influence gave it a penitential character. By the twelfth century a compromise was effected so that it became a time of joyful penance. Holiday food preparations begin in Advent. Each ethnic group has its own particular Advent and Christmas customs, and food is a large part of all of them. For example, the Italians bake twelve varieties of cookies, one for each of the Twelve Days of Christmas (cf. Barolini, p. 20).

Christmas

History of the Feast

In the year 312, under the Emperor Constantine, the Church was at last free from persecution. About the middle of the fourth century, she established a special feast to commemorate the birth of Christ. In 386, St. John Chrysostom wrote that Julian had made an extensive investigation of the correct birthday of Christ and found that the Western churches all considered December 25 to be the Nativity date, although the Eastern churches claimed January 6. Other opinions said the birth of Christ should be observed on April 20, May 20, March 29, or September 29. Basing his opinion on the majority, Pope Julian decreed the feast for December 25 (Hottes, p. 16).

By the Middle Ages, this feast acquired the popular name of Christmas, the Mass of Christ. Quickly it became one of the most joyous feasts of the liturgical year, and was celebrated happily in the churches and in the homes.

From the early Middle Ages, the twelve days from the Nativity of Our Lord to the Epiphany (January 6) were kept as a festive season. Although these twelve days are dominated by Christmas, they also contain other liturgical feasts to increase the spirit of joy and celebration.

Fowl, both wild and tame, were popular Christmas gifts and payments in the Middle Ages, and were often presented live to be kept in special pens and fed on such delicacies as raisins and milk until they were needed in the kitchen. This custom, plus the difficulties of keeping more than the breeding stock of the larger animals, set a pattern of Christmas eating that is followed to this day. Thus, fowl are the main dishes for Christmas dinner in most parts of Europe. In the Pacific Island regions, suckling pig is the Christmas meat, while lamb is common in Iceland, Spain, Sardinia, and New Zealand.

Wild turkeys were still plentiful in New England when the Pilgrim Fathers caught some for their first Thanksgiving dinner in 1621. Domesticated turkeys had been found by explorers in Mexico and Central America a century earlier and were first imported to Spain in 1498. The earliest written record of turkeys' success in England came in 1541, when Archbishop Cranmer, attempting to limit the gluttony of the higher clergy, laid down a list of "greater fowls," among them turkey-cocks, of which only one was permitted in a dish (Poole, p. 62).

Great English Christmas pies were majestic constructions. In the Middle Ages, a plain flour-and-water crust was originally wrapped around meat to keep it from drying out during baking. Soon, the pies began to be baked larger and larger. One pie baked for Sir Henry Grey was nine feet in circumference and weighed 165 pounds. It was served from a special cart built to carry it (Hottes, p. 104).

Do you remember Little Jack Horner, who sat in a corner, eating his Christmas pie? He put in his thumb and pulled out a plum and said, "What a good boy am I."

Well, the plum Jack found was not the fruit. Jack was steward to the last Abbot of Glastonbury. He was entrusted with delivering a Christmas pie from the abbot to King Henry VIII in London. During the journey, he looked under the pie crust and found the deeds to several manor houses in the county of Somerset. He helped himself to the papers of the Manor of Mells, which remained in the Horner family for some years afterward (Poole, p. 102).

William the Conqueror was crowned on Christmas Day 1066. A member of his domestic staff, Robert Argyllon, is credited with originating the forebear of today's plum pudding. The same pudding was served at the manor of Addington in Surrey and at the royal table at coronations up through the coronation of George IV in 1820.

The Medieval Feast

Before the medieval feast, the guests were served the wassail bowl to awaken their appetites. Our Saxon ancestors often quaffed their ale from the skulls of their enemies. Rowena, the daughter of Hengist, brought a bowl of wine to Prince Vortigern and saluted him by saying, *"Wass heil."* He answered back, *"Drinc heile,"* and soon married the young lady. (In modern English, we would translate *Wass heil* loosely as "Here's to you.") The bowl itself was a graceful design, often ornamented with the shape of leaves. Wassail became a traditional mixture, usually of hot ale, sugar, and spices. Those who could afford it used a rich wine. Apples were floated on the surface and were sometimes referred to as lamb's wool. Other old writers called the whole decoction lamb's wool, or "old man's beard." Still others named it church ale from the custom of the church to sell this drink around Christmas time to raise alms for the poor.

The feast itself consisted of a number of traditional dishes. The boar's head was always a popular course. The wild pig was honored as having taught mankind how to plow. (In later centuries, when the wild pig had become scarce, the boar's head was made from a domesticated pig, with elaborate instructions given on how to make fake tusks.) The peacock was a kingly dish. An old manuscript cookbook of 1430 gives directions for cooking the bird and serving it resplendent in its brilliant plumage. The bird was sometimes made into a pie with its head sticking out of one side of the crust and the tail from the other. Sometimes a sponge was saturated with spirits and placed in the beak. This was lighted as the dish was ceremoniously served.

At the end of each course, interesting sugar statues, called "subtleties," were placed on the table. These depicted biblical scenes such as the Wise Men and the Holy Family. The feast continued from about three in the afternoon until midnight, when our gluttonous forefathers finished their meal with pheasants, oysters, and several big bowls of steaming hot punch.

Then, as today, pastimes were played. One of the favorites was called Snapdragon. Guests were to snatch objects out of burning brandy and pop them into their mouths. The word snapdragon is possibly derived from *Schnapps*, "liquor," and *Drache*, "dragon" (Hottes, p. 116).

Christmas Toasts

From early days, it was common to float things in a bowl of warm liquor. Sometimes this was fruit, such as the apples in wassail, or the raisins in snapdragon. Sometimes this was a piece of toasted bread. An old story tells that one day a favorite young lady of the court fell into a pool, whereupon one of the young men standing around suggested that all the young gallants take a drink of the water in the pool. Another young man quickly remarked that he preferred the toast to the liquor, and thereupon jumped in the pool and pressed a delicious kiss upon the young lady's lips. Hence, the origin of the toast (Hottes, p. 167).

It is an old British custom to drink to an absent person after dinner, and such a person was known as the toast. Gradually the meaning changed to signify anything that was commemorated. Today, a Christmas toast is drunk in many cultures.

Christmas Breads

Bread has been symbolic of Christ from earliest times. The very name Bethlehem means "house of bread." Christ the Bread of angels has been honored with special Christmas bread in almost every European country. Early Christians brought their bread to the altar at the offertory procession. Some of it was used for the Sacrifice; some was blessed and taken home. In Germany, Christollen is baked in a shape evocative of the Child in swaddling clothes. The Greek spiced bread sometimes has a small infant doll baked in it, symbolic of the Child Jesus. Other special Christmas breads are discussed in the section on customs from the various countries.

Modern Customs

In American homes today, we celebrate with symbols and customs from many countries: the Christmas tree from Germany, the crib from Italy, Santa Claus from Holland, lights in the windows, carols, presents, and so on. Each nation had gradually developed its own special customs regarding the Christmas foods.

The traditional American meal is basically English in origin although the English goose or capon has been supplanted by turkey and many side dishes claim other national origins. In the early days of our country, however. Christmas was not as popular as it is today. The Puritans were bitterly opposed to the celebration of it, and in 1659 in Massachusetts a law was passed outlawing the day. This law remained in force for twenty-two years, and Christmas was not a legal holiday until late in the first half of the nineteenth century (Hottes, p. 296).

Other Christmas traditions call for special, sweeter desserts and varied and fancy breads and cakes. The baking of special breads is an ancient tradition of thanksgiving for the grain harvest. In Ireland, this custom called forth a special name for the Holy Night, the "Night of Cakes" (*Oidhche na ceapairi*). This joyful feast also became a favorite occasion for drinking pleasant and light alcoholic beverages. Only in recent years has a stronger liquor replaced the ales, ciders, and wines of the past (Kaufman, p. 37).

Many European and South American countries make dolls of sweet yeast dough to delight children at Christmas breakfasts and dinners. In Ecuador and Guatemala, these carefully modeled dolls are trimmed with brilliantly colored sugar icing, and in Peru bright feather headdresses are often added. In Finland, the dolls are in the form of faces called *Pullaukkoja*. The Swiss version is called *Grittibanz*, and the faces vary in size up to two feet (Sheraton, p. 5).

Some of the many traditional foods and food customs worldwide are discussed here. But to adequately describe the Catholic food customs of Christmas, we would have to enter millions of homes, for each lends its own flavor to the traditions of the area.

In Argentina, Christmas is in midsummer. After early Mass, Christmas dinner may be served in the garden. The table is decorated with rosebuds and jessamine and a suckling pig. *Niños envueltos* (children wrapped up) is one entrée. This dish consists of pieces of steak about three inches square, rolled and stuffed with minced meat seasoned with olives, hard-boiled eggs, and spices. The *pièce de resistance* is a roasted peacock (Hottes, p. 202).

The Armenian villagers in Persia and India fasted for a week before Christmas and on the last day ate no food at all. After communion on Christmas Eve, the people return home to break their fast. *Pilav*, a rice food, is eaten for the evening meal, after which the children go to the housetops and hang their handkerchiefs over the roof in hopes of getting raisins, fried wheat, or money. This is the evening for engaged young men to present their fiancées with a traditional gift: a tray with twelve pieces of cake, a candle, nine eggs, some raisins, a plate of *halva* (a kind of sweet meat) and a box of henna with which to paint their hair and hands. In some places, the evening meal is fried fish, lettuce, and boiled spinach, for the people believe Mary ate spinach on the Eve of Christ's birth. The people leave for church an hour before dawn, and the service is not over until 10:30. The fasting often caused people to faint from hunger during the service. The Christmas observance lasts three days ending on Ladies Day, on which the Armenians give and receive calls (Hottes, p. 204).

In Brazil, the Christmas season is in midsummer and is celebrated with fireworks, picnics, and other summertime diversions. It is doubly appreciated by the young folk because it comes at the close of school and ushers in the holidays.

In Bulgaria, *medeni kurabii*, honey cookies, are a traditional Christmas treat.

In the Central African Republic, there is no such thing as a traditional Christmas dinner. The celebration in this country is on Christmas Eve. In this part of Africa, the holiday is primarily for the children. At noon, the children eat a large meal. The evening celebration has no meat, cheese, or vegetable dishes. The children gather in one of the neighborhood homes for tea. This is the one night of the year that the children can eat as many sweets as they like. Tea is served hot with milk and sugar. A fruit *samba* (punch), *makaras* (small cakes), and bonbons are served. The children gather around the Christmas crib and sing hymns and songs. The customs in this region of Africa are influenced greatly by those of France because it was French missionaries who first evangelized there.

At the Christmas fiesta in Andacolla, Chile, the miraculous statue of the Virgin del Rosario is honored by dancers and a large procession. Stalls along the streets sell dolls, trinkets, and hot *empañadas* (individual meat pies). *Chicha* (a fermented drink) is enjoyed by all (Hottes, p. 215).

In China, the Christmas festival was known as *Sheng Dan Jieh*, the holy Birth Festival. Beautiful paper decorations adorned the churches and homes. The tree was decorated with paper flowers, colored chains, and snowflakes (Hottes, p. 216). Christmas was celebrated as one of the four first-class feast days, and families served a rich banquet.

In Costa Rica, the *presipios* (manger scenes) are called *portals*. Sometimes an entire room of the home is filled with these replicas of holy scenes, some containing hundreds of figures, and at Christmas time the people visit from house to house to see each one (Hottes, p. 217). Special Christmas sweets are set out for visitors.

Everyone fasted on Christmas eve in Bohemia (the former western province of Czechoslovakia) until supper, which consisted of seven courses. Enough was prepared to make certain there were plenty of leftovers to feed to the family pigs. The children were delighted to see the Golden Pigs appear on the walls and ceiling (reflections of lighted candles caused this illusion.) On Christmas day the family gathered around the manger scene and sang Christmas carols. Then they began a celebration with feasting that lasted for three days.

Christmas Eve is the festive time in Denmark. Christmas dinner is served about six in the evening, and the menu is rice in which a whole almond is cooked. The person who gets the almond in his portion receives a prize. Then comes roast goose stuffed with prunes and apples, sugar-browned potatoes, red cabbage, and currant jelly. The head of the house gives a toast with delicious claret. Apple cakes covered with whipped cream and all kinds of fruits and nuts are served for dessert. After dinner, presents are distributed and the family enjoys singing carols around the tree. Late in the evening, tea, sandwiches, and Christmas cakes and cookies are served, including pink marzipan Christmas pigs. Christmas day is a day for visiting and hospitality.

Before Christmas Eve dinner was served, many Danish families used to take a bowl of rice and milk to the attic for *Jule-nissen*, the Christmas elf. This little old man, dressed in gray with a painted red nightcap, was a friend indeed to those who loved kindness and peace, and he played all sort of tricks on those who bred contention in the family (Hottes, p. 222).

Christmas is so much a time of feasting in England that it is difficult to know where to begin and end a discussion of all the good things served at this season. From earliest times, even in Roman days, it was common to bake Yule Dough. This was generally a flat cake in the shape of a baby that bakers presented to their customers. Mince pie has always represented the choicest, spiciest productions of the East, and it symbolizes the gifts of the wise men to the Child Jesus.

Mince pies were first baked in the form of the manger, and the old books called the upper crust of the pie its coffin. If a lattice crust was used, it represented the hayrack of the stable. As early as 1596, the pies were popular under the name of mutton pies, and later neats' tongues were used. Their original name was *shrid pye* (shredded pie). During the time of the Reformation, many of the old writers of religious tracts called the pies "idolatrie in crust." One writer said, "Such pye is an hodge-podge of superstition, Popery, the devil and all its works" (Hottes, p. 185).

In modern England, the Christmas spirit started before the actual day on "stir-up Sunday" (the Sunday that falls closest to St. Andrew's Day in November) with young folk in the kitchen in the evenings getting ready the plum puddings to be distributed among their poorer brothers and sisters. One night was spent chopping the fruits and suet; the next was devoted to stirring the contents. Each of the group had to give a stir for good luck. Then came a long evening when the puddings were put in cloth and boiled in large coppers. The boys took turns stoking the fires under the coppers. Christmas songs were sung and stories were told until the puddings were boiled long enough.

On Christmas evening, after church at eleven P.M,. companies of "waits," or carol singers, went from home to home. After the songs, a silver offering exchanged hands, and coffee and cakes were given the singers to warm their whistles. Before the household settled down and the guests departed, a huge pitcher of "Tom and Jerry" went around. At last, about three A.M. the house was hushed in slumber (Hottes, p. 227).

After Christmas breakfast, the family enjoyed the presents under the Christmas tree. Then the youths delivered the plum puddings, often with a bright new shilling or charm inside. And always, there was a sprig of holly on top to keep away the witches. The young ladies and their beaux then returned home for more "Tom and Jerry" before lunch. After supper, the plum pudding was brought in alight with spirits. The pudding contained a thimble, a button, and a bright shilling, each with its prophecy for the coming year. A toast of champagne ended the meal, and the family played games until bedtime.

In many parts of rural England years ago it was the custom to have a hodening horse go from house to house. The head of the animal was carved from wood; it was made as grotesque as possible. Two boys or young men beneath a sheet formed the horse. This horse and his followers went about scaring the families, after which they expected to be invited in for a treat of cakes and cider (Hottes, p. 230).

In Fiji, Christmas feasting is done in the open air around an enormous pit barbecue called a *lovo*. One of the cold side dishes usually served is called *kakoda*. It is marinated raw fish.

A bath was part of the Christmas celebration in Finland. First the house was cleaned thoroughly, and straw was spread on the floor where the children would sleep in remembrance of the Holy Child in the manger. Then, just before Christmas Eve, the whole family took a Finnish bath, or sauna. After the bath, a supper was eaten of barley porridge mixed with almonds, cream, and sugar. Stockfish and prune tarts added to the festivity of the meal. After church on Christmas day, families enjoyed a meal of Christmas ham and spent the rest of the afternoon resting, singing carols, and reading the Bible (Hottes, p. 233).

Christmas Eve is a fête in France. Cafes are open all night for the Christmas *Reveillon*, or supper after midnight. After Mass, the people go with their families to the cafés or return home for a feast of brown-baked ham, roast chickens, salads, cake, fruit, bonbons, and wine. The traditional completion to this meal is the rich chocolate roll called the *Buche de Noël*, a cake baked in the form of a Christmas log. Even the animals enjoy the feast, and "church bread" is given to them in their stalls.

In the Provence region, a traditional meatless feast is held which utilizes the superb garlic and herbs grown in the dry sunshine of Southern France. The meal begins with a simple soup called *aigo bouillido*, which literally translates to boiling water. Next comes artichoke with anchovy sauce, snails, eels, and a salad. Then come thirteen traditional items of fruits, nuts and sweets.

Christmarkt, or Fair, starts on December 6 in Germany. The streets are filled with Christmas spirit; booths sell cookies, candies, trees, and toys. After church on Christmas Eve, the families return home to celebrate. One popular dish is *Karpfen in Bier* (carp in beer), and family members save one of the fishes' large scales to bring luck in the coming year.

Gingerbreads were among the first cakes to be made for Christmas celebrations. Some of the earliest were no more than dry white bread crumbs mixed with spice and honey to form a stiff paste which could be molded and decorated. Most of the recipes used today are simple ones, although the decorations may be elaborate. Germany's many types of *Lebkuchen* and *Pfefferkuchen* are among the most lavish, and are fashioned into all kinds of fancy cakes. "Leb" comes from the Latin *libum*, a consecrated cake used in Roman religious ceremonies. Hence, the Lebkuchen are, in Germany, almost sacred cakes.

One of the many traditional Christmas cookies in Germany is the *Springerle*, embossed anise-scented cookies. These cookies actually date back to the midwinter pagan celebration of *Julfest*. Germanic tribes sacrificed animals to their gods. Poor people could not afford to slaughter their animals, so they offered token sacrifices of animal-shaped cookies. The name Springerle is from the German for a vaulting horse (or rabbit in diminutive). In Christian times, the *Reitersmann* — a man riding a horse — became one of the most popular forms of these ornamental cookie molds (mounted on a curved board or rolling pin).

In Greek homes, special loaves of bread (*Christopsomo*) are baked for Christmas and marked with a cross on the top. A silver coin is hidden in the loaf. The housewife fumigates the house with frankincense, and then she and her husband break the bread into small pieces. The first piece goes to St. Basil, the Holy Virgin, or the patron saint whose icon is in the house. The second piece is for the house, the third for the animals, and the fourth for inanimate property. The rest of the loaf is divided among the family, who dip their portion in wine before eating it. The one who finds the coin will have good luck through the year. He takes the coin and buys a candle for the church. After the evening meal, the table is not cleared but left in hopes that St. Basil may come to partake of the remains.

There are countless recipes for the light, fragrant Christmas shortbread made in Greece. It is of ancient origin, and is said to have been mentioned by St. John Chrysostom in one of his sermons. Today it is usually made in the form of individual cookies, each spiked with a clove to represent the gift of spices which the wise men brought to the Infant Christ. Another traditional Greek cookie, the *diples*, refers to the diapers or swaddling clothes of the Christ Child.

In Holland, the eve of St. Nicholas's feast is a special celebration. St. Nicholas and his servant, a little Moor named Black Pete, come and question the children as to whether or not they have been good the preceding year. Then the children place their wooden shoes filled with hay for St. Nicholas's horse in front of the fireplace. After the children are put to bed, the adults sit around the table and have tea and *speculaas* (hard cookies) as they enjoy their presents. After the packages have been opened, they eat *letterbanket*, chocolates and cakes made in the form of an initial, and drink hot punch or chocolate milk. Additionally, a dish of boiled chestnuts is brought in, which all enjoy eating with butter and salt (Hottes, p. 244). In Holland, Christmas day is generally devoted to church and social visiting.

At Christmas, Catholics in Bangalore, India, traditionally enjoy Banana *Halwa, Chakulies,* Coconut Toffee, *Dhole Dhole, Gingelly Ladoos, Gulio* Marbles, Sweet Puffs, *Sukkur Undae, Kokisan, Kulkuls,* and Milk Toffee.

During penal days in Ireland, the people had no churches and priests remained in hiding. On Christmas Eve, the faithful placed burning candles in the window so that any priest who happened to be in the vicinity would be guided to their homes through the dark night. The sturdy Irish Catholics told the English soldiers that the candles were a symbol so that Jesus and Mary, looking for a place to stay, would know they were welcome. The soldiers, finding the superstition harmless, did not bother to suppress it. Guided by the flickering lights, the rebel priests would enter the homes silently. After offering Mass, the family fed the priest, who was soon on his way.

Italians celebrated Christmas for three weeks from the Novena (eight days before Christmas) until the Twelfth Night. The twenty-four hours before Christmas Eve, everyone fasts — and then an elaborate banquet is served. Different areas of the country, and even single towns, have long held traditions of eating particular dishes on Christmas Eve. In a number of places, it is traditional to eat seven fish dishes. In Bologna, Christmas dinner always begins with tortellini. According to a romantic local legend, these little rings of deliciously stuffed dough were the invention of a lovelorn cook who, catching sight of his master's wife sleeping naked, cooked and served pasta fashioned in the shape of her navel as a token of his hopeless passion (Poole, p. 27).

Sweets are popular with the Italians, and there are literally hundreds of cakes, cookies, and other desserts that are traditional for one feast or another.

From earliest times, Magi cakes were popular in Italy. These took the place of visiting cards and were exchanged between friends. The larger the cake, the better. Once the Prince of Borghese received a Magi Cake adorned with his coat of arms, which was six meters long (Hottes, p. 195).

In Africa, there are many tribes; there are at least seventy in Kenya alone. Each tribe has its own traditions, but among Catholics Christmas is a time for family get-togethers and visits. In Kenya, the celebration lasts from Christmas Eve until January 1, and businesses close during the entire week. People often have to travel long distances to their mission churches for midnight Mass. At the mission, they set up camp and sleep in the open air by campfires. The people join in Christmas songs and prayers, and after midnight Mass they dance, sing, visit, tell stories, and share food. Peanut soup is a favorite Kenyan recipe.

On Christmas night, Lithuanians served a twelve-course dinner in honor of the Twelve Apostles.

In Mexico, the houses are decorated and ready for guests by December 16. From this night until Christmas, the people will have parties and the traditional *posadas*. The posadas commemorate the journey of Mary and Joseph and their attempt to find lodging. Mary, Joseph, and a group of pilgrims carrying candles wend their way in procession from house to house, knocking and seeking admittance. Time after time they are told, "There is no room." At last, they arrive at the home that is prepared for the party that will ensue after the holy couple is allowed to come in and the litany is said by all. The party on the last night, Christmas Eve, is the most lavish of all. The home altar is beautifully decorated, and the Infant Jesus is found in a moss-lined crib. There is singing, and much liquor and food. Everyone dances and parties until time for midnight Mass. One feature of this party is a *piñata*, a large container filled with candy, gum, small toys, and other gifts. The piñata is hung from the ceiling. The children gather around and take turns being blindfolded and trying to break the piñata. At last a lucky hit is made, and all scramble to retrieve their share of the goodies.

Buñuelos, or fritters, are a traditional staple both for Christmas and for Lent. These are reminiscent of Arab sweets brought to Mexico during the Spanish conquest and adopted by the natives (Quintana, p. 71).

Tamales, a form of savory pie, are traditional Mexican and American Southwest fare. The *tamalada* is a community or family get-together to make the delicious tamales in large quantities for Christmas eating and sharing.

In Nigeria, after midnight Mass, the people began to play and shout, throwing firecrackers in the air. They wear masks and special outfits and stay up drinking, singing, and dancing. Food is often one of the main presents the people exchange. A festive dinner may include *obe didin* (goat stew), *moi moi* (*moyin-moyin*), and *jollof* rice.

Preparations for Christmas begin months in advance in Norway. Butchering is done in October and November; several kinds of sausages are made, as well as meat that is cured for the entire year. An entire year's supply of some baked goods is also made. There is *flad Brod*, a thin bread made from oat flour. There are waffles, and *lefse*, made of mashed potatoes, salt, cream, and flour, rolled thin like a pie crust and baked on a griddle, to be served buttered with syrup. Dozens of kinds of cheese are made and the choicest put away for Christmas.

In Norway, as in all Scandinavian countries, sheafs of grain were tied to poles and placed in front of the houses as Christmas treats for the birds.

On Christmas Eve, a huge roast beef was served with *rome grod*, a rice mush made with cream. *Kringler*, a yeast dough twisted, frosted with brown sugar, and flavored with cardamon, was a special feature of the meal. Other Norwegian foods included pickled pig's head, pickled herring, broiled mutton and veal, a suckling pig, and a special keg of Christmas beer. Before bedtime, there was Yule porridge made of milk, rice, and cinnamon.

On Christmas day, the Yule table is fixed, not for the regular meals but for the many friends that will visit. After church on Christmas day, a fish dinner is served, with fish soup and all the varieties of baked, fried, and broiled fish that one can imagine. All day the Yule table is raided. The roast dinner is prefaced with a fruit soup and the Christmas sausage that has been frozen since its mixing (Hottes, p. 266).

Christmas Eve is a fast day in Poland until the evening meal. Baskets of food are either taken to church during the day for a blessing, or the priest comes to the home to bless the food that will be eaten that evening. As soon as the evening star appears, the feasting begins. Oplatek is a thin rice wafer stamped with sacred figures and blessed by the priest. Wafers are broken and eaten by all at the table, as they exchange good wishes and honor those family members who are away from home. Straw is scattered under the table, and one chair is left vacant for the Holy Child. A large meal of fish, rye mush, currants, and almonds is served.

In Puerto Rico, a *batea*, or large tub, is filled with candy made from rice, coconuts, raisins, sugar, and cinnamon. This is called *Arocco con dulce*. Chocolate and coffee are served with the candy (Hottes, p. 271). Christmas dinner usually includes *lechón asado* (roasted pork), *pasteles* (similar to a tamale, made of green bananas), and *arroz con gandules* (rice with pigeon peas.)

In the old pre-communist days in Rumania, on *Nosterea Domnului Isus* (Christmas Eve), everyone ate a special cake called a *turta*. It was made of many layers of thinly rolled dough, filled with melted sugar or honey, ground walnuts or hemp seed. The dough was prepared the night before and taken into the garden where a tree ceremony was enacted by the husband and wife to insure the fruitfulness of the trees. The husband would go from tree to tree, threatening to cut each one down. The wife would stand in front of the tree saying, "Spare this tree for next year it will be as heavy with fruit as my hands are with dough." The turta, with its thin coats of rolled dough, represents the swaddling clothes of the Infant Jesus. Another special Christmas cake was made which contained nuts and raisins, and the Christmas supper was generally a pork roast cooked with sauerkraut.

In Old Russia before the revolution, the Christmas-eve supper began when the evening star appeared. The table was covered with straw, and a samovar was placed on the table with fish and cakes. The feast began by dividing the blessed wafer. After midnight Mass, the families returned home to enjoy the presents under their tree. The Christmas dinner the next day was a special meal. Although there was no meat, there was cold fish, cold vegetable soup with mushrooms, and little rice cakes resembling pies (Hottes, p. 273).

In some parts of Scotland, oatcakes — impressed with a cross and called Yule-bannocks — are baked at daybreak on Christmas morning in honor of the Virgin's delivery.

In Spain, sea bream (porgy) are the traditional Christmas Eve fare, although each region has its own special way of cooking the fish. In the old days in Spain, Christmas dinner was often eaten in church.

In Sweden, pork plays a great role at Christmas time. The Christmas-day meal is a suckling pig roasted whole with a red apple in its mouth. All kinds of tempting small cakes are made. A Swedish hostess at Christmas time expects to offer at least six different kinds of attractive cakes with coffee. There are ginger snaps, ginger cake, Siamese twins, goats, almond rings, currant cookies, macaroons, and a round, braided loaf of especially good sweet white bread, colored yellow with saffron and filled with raisins and citron. Little puff pastries are made in the form of conch-shells and filled with preserves made from a berry that grows only within the Arctic Circle. In Sweden, as in many of the Scandinavian countries, huge sheaves of grain are placed outside as edible Christmas trees for the birds.

The Syrian Christmas is not a period of merrymaking and exchanging of gifts, but a season of prayer and quiet rejoicing. The main feature of Christmas day is the holiday dinner at which are served chicken, oranges, nuts, and Turkish Delight.

In the Tyrol, it is an old custom to leave a large bowl of milk in front of the picture of the Holy Family. Each member of the family places a spoon against the edge of the bowl. Then the family leaves for Mass. On their return, the children race to see which spoon has been moved by the Blessed Virgin as she fed the Holy Infant. That person will have good luck the coming year.

Before Christmas, the Ukrainian people used to fast for thirty-nine days to prepare for the Nativity. On Christmas Eve the long fast was broken with a sumptuous twelve-course dinner, one course served in memory of each of the Twelve Apostles. In some places there is a custom of eating a bowl of porridge and honey with fruit to represent the Holy Crib. The dish is called *Koutia*. First the porridge is put in as the straw of the manger. Then each person helps himself to fruit, symbolizing the Babe, with honey representing the Spirit.

Christmas dinners in the United States are as varied as the ethnic backgrounds of the families eating them. For example, in my part of the country tamales are a traditional Christmas dish among those of Mexican descent while gumbo is often served by many from East Texas and Louisiana and by those of African heritage. Gumbo, as a matter of fact, is a Bantu word for okra, a vegetable that is often, but not always, used in the dish. One dish that is generally found on many American tables, however, is cranberry sauce. The cranberry is a fruit native to our country. Varieties of wild cranberries are found in Europe and Asia, but the American variety is the only species ever to be successfully cultivated.

One purely American Christmas confection is the popcorn ball, which can be found served from large bowls or hung by ribbons or wires from the Christmas tree.

In the former Yugoslavia, a *Polaznik*, or young man admired by the family, was usually invited to join the family for Christmas. He was a special guest of the day and had to taste all the holiday dainties. When he left in the evening, he was given a gift for bringing good luck to the family (Hottes, p. 251). Christmas dinner took much preparation. A thick soup called *chorba* came first. A whole pig was the main dish. The *chestnitea*, or Christmas cake, was cut into as many pieces as there were persons present. A silver coin hidden inside brought good luck to the finder. Sometimes other small trinkets were baked in the cake, and the objects told the future for the young men and women of the family. On Christmas afternoon, the young men rode their horses up and down the streets, singing and firing their pistols to express happiness.

Peanut Soup

- 4 beef (or chicken) bouillon cubes
- 1 qt. water
- 2 or 3 green onions with tops, chopped
- 1 c. raw peanuts, ground into a fine powder*
- 1 medium carrot, diced
- 1/4 c. rice
- 1/4 tsp. ground red pepper

Place all ingredients in a heavy 2-3-qt. saucepan. Bring to a boil. Reduce heat, cover and simmer about 30 minutes until rice is tender. Add water if soup becomes too thick.

Yield: serves 4.

I grind peanuts in a coffee grinder; a blender will do fine.

Aigo Bouillido (Boiling Water)

- 2 large cloves garlic
- 1 tbsp. olive oil
- 1 bay leaf
- 1 tsp. salt
- 4 c. water
- 2 eggs

Boil all ingredients except eggs for about 15 minutes. Break the eggs into a soup tureen and pour the boiling water over them. Beat for a few moments with a wooden spoon.

Yield: serves 4.

Obe Didin **(Fried Stew)**

- 1 8-oz. can tomato sauce
- 1 6-oz.can tomato paste
- 1/4 c. palm oil (vegetable oil may be substituted)
- 1/2 tsp. coarse ground pepper
- 1 small onion, sliced
- salt to taste
- 2 lbs. meat
- oil to fry meat

Combine tomato paste, sauce, onion, pepper, oil, and simmer.

In Nigeria, the stew is made of fresh goat or ram. (It is still delicious with beef substituted for the goat.) The intestines are cleaned and boiled, then fried in oil. The meat is cut into chunks and fried in oil to sear and brown the outside. The partially cooked meat is then put into the tomato-pepper sauce and cooked, covered, over low heat until done, about 30 minutes. Stir to prevent scorching. The meat is taken out of the sauce and put on a plate to serve. The sauce is put in a separate dish, for use as a gravy.

Yield: serves 4 to 6.

— Juliana Tubi

Pirohy (Polish: Pirógi) **(Egg Dumplings)**

- 1 c. flour
- 1 egg
- 4 tbsp. water
- cheese, potato, or sauerkraut filling (next page)

Mix flour and egg with enough water to make a soft dough. Knead well. Roll out on floured board until thin. Cut into three-inch squares. Place one tsp. filling (next page) on each square. Fold in half, making a triangle. Pinch edges well to keep filling inside. Drop into boiling salted water and cook until dumplings rise to surface. Cook five minutes longer. Rinse in colander with hot water. Drain. Pour melted butter over dumplings and serve.

Pirohy **Fillings:**

Cheese Filling:
- 1/2 c. dry cottage cheese
- 1 egg yolk
- 1 tsp. butter
- pinch salt

Potato Filling:
- 1 large potato, cooked and mashed.
- 1 tablespoon butter
- grated cheese to taste

Sauerkraut Filling:
- small can sauerkraut
- small onion, diced

Drain and rinse sauerkraut in cold water. Brown diced onion in margarine and add to sauerkraut. Cook for a few minutes.

Marzipan (Almond Paste)

- 2 3/4 c. ground almonds
- 2 c. confectioners' sugar
- rose water, orange juice, or lemon juice

Work the almonds and sugar into a firm paste with just enough liquid to make it pliable. Put the paste in a small saucepan and stir it over a low heat until it no longer sticks to the sides of the pan. Turn onto a sugar-dusted board. Shape into figures for candy. These may be left lightly covered in a warm place to dry a little.

Yield: 1 pound.

This is the traditional way to make marzipan. Your grocery store may have it packaged ready-made in the section devoted to baking.

Christmas Goose

- 1 goose (6-8 lbs.)
- 1/4 c. butter or margarine
- 1 large onion, chopped fine
- 4 c. fresh white or whole-wheat bread crumbs
- 4 leaves fresh sage, minced, or 1/2 tsp. dried sage
- 1/8 tsp. dried oregano
- 1 tsp. salt
- black pepper to taste

Clean the goose and prepare for stuffing. In a small pan, melt the butter and fry the onion gently until clear. Mix the onions and butter with the bread crumbs, oregano, and sage. Season with salt and pepper.

Stuff the goose with the bread mixture. Truss and roast. Roast at 400 degrees for the first fifteen minutes. Then reduce heat to 325 and roast for an additional 3 1/2 to 4 hours for a 6-8 lb. goose. Follow cooking chart for a larger bird.

Yield: serves 4 to 6.

Leche Flan (Caramel Custard)

- 1 c. brown sugar
- 2 c. milk
- 8 egg yolks
- 1 c. granulated sugar
- grated rind of 1 lemon
- 1/4 tsp. grated nutmeg

Scald the milk. Beat eggs and sugar together and gradually beat in the milk. Add the lemon rind and nutmeg and mix thoroughly.

Dissolve the brown sugar in 1/4 c. water in a small saucepan over low heat, then boil the syrup briskly until it caramelizes. Do not let the caramel become too dark or it will be bitter. Pour the caramel into a shallow, well-buttered ovenproof dish or into several small custard cups.

Pour the custard over the caramel. Stand the dish in a larger baking tray and pour water into the outer container until it comes about halfway up the sides of the custard dish. Bake in preheated oven at low heat (275 degrees) for about an hour, or until the custard has set.

Cool the custard before turning it out of the mold, caramel side up. Lucky coins wrapped in aluminum foil can be pressed into the cold custard before unmolding.

Yield: serves 4 to 6.

Boiled Custard

- 3/4 c. sugar
- 1/4 tsp. salt
- 4 tbsp. (rounded) flour
- 1 qt. cold milk
- 4 eggs, separated
- 1 tsp. vanilla
- 1/2 pt. whipping cream, whipped

Sift together first three ingredients. Pour one qt. cold milk gradually into dry ingredients, stirring well. Beat egg yolks and stir into mixture. Put on low heat and cook, stirring constantly until thick. Beat egg whites until stiff. Pour hot custard over whites and beat together. Add vanilla. Before serving, fold in whipping cream. Serve alone or over mince or apple pie.

Yield: 1 quart.

— Margaret McDougle

Hogmany

- 1 c. honey
- 2 c. heavy sweet cream
- 2 c. Scotch whiskey

Heat honey over low heat and when it thins, stir in the cream. Remove from heat and slowly stir in the whiskey. Serve hot in mugs.

Yield: serves 4 to 6.

Lamb's Wool

- 1 bottle sweet white wine
- 2 pints ale
- 6 apples
- 42 whole cloves
- 1/4 tsp. ground nutmeg
- 1 tbsp. butter or margarine
- 3 tbsp. brown sugar

Stick the cloves in the apples and bake until very soft, about 40 minutes at 350 degrees. Scoop out the pulp and put in a bowl. Add the sugar, nutmeg, and butter. Pour the wine and ale into a pan and heat just to boiling. Float apple mixture on top and serve in toddy glasses.

Yield: 10 to 12.

— adapted from Leo Knowles

Wassail

- 2 qts. apple cider
- 2 c. pineapple juice
- 1 1/2 c. orange juice
- 1/2 c. lemon juice
- 1 c. sugar
- 2 sticks whole cinnamon
- 1 tsp. whole cloves

Combine ingredients and bring to a boil. Serve hot. Garnish with cinnamon sticks if desired.

Wassail is one of those things that good cooks argue about the traditional components of. Our version is simple and quick. Check entries in a number of cookbooks for interesting variations.

Yield: serves 6 to 10.

Cauliflower Relish

- 1 head cauliflower
- 1 tsp. dill seed, or fresh dill
- 1 tsp. salt
- 1 or 2 small hot peppers
- vinegar

Boil head of cauliflower until just tender. Separate into flowerlets, reserving water. Pack into a clean glass jar. Add 1 tsp. dill seed or, preferably, several fresh heads of dill, 1 tsp. salt, and one or two small fresh red chilis or other hot peppers, cut into fourths and with seeds removed. Fill jar 2/3 full with plain white vinegar, and complete with the water reserved from boiling the cauliflower. Seal and store in refrigerator at least a week prior to eating.

— adapted from a recipe from the 1600s

Cranberry Sauce

- 1 c. water
- 1 c. sugar
- 3 c. fresh or frozen cranberries

Combine water and sugar in saucepan and stir to dissolve sugar. Bring to a boil and add cranberries, reducing heat to medium low. Cook until skins pop. Cool at room temperature. Refrigerate till firm.

Yield: two and one-half cups.

Cranberry-Orange Relish

- 1 c. water
- 1 c. sugar
- 3 c. fresh or frozen cranberries
- 1/2 c. chopped pecans (or walnuts)
- 3 large oranges

Boil the water and sugar. Add cranberries and cook over low heat until the skins pop. Remove from heat. Add pecans. Peel and section oranges and cut into small pieces. Add to cranberry mixture. Refrigerate.

Yield: about three cups.

Squash Bake

- 3 pkgs. frozen yellow squash, cooked according to directions
- 2 eggs, well beaten
- 1/2 c. Ritz cracker crumbs
- 4 tbsp. margarine, melted
- 1 c. grated cheese
- 1/2 tsp. Italian seasoning
- 1/2 c. chopped onion
- 1/2 tsp. garlic powder
- 1/2 tsp. black pepper
- 1 tsp. salt or to taste

With a potato masher, mash squash and add well-beaten eggs. Cream mixture well. Add cracker crumbs, margarine, part of cheese, Italian seasoning, onion, pepper, salt, and garlic powder. Pour into a lightly greased baking dish. Sprinkle top with remaining cheese. Bake at 325 degrees about 20 to 30 minutes.

Yield: Serves six to eight.

— Mildred Kerr

Sweet Potatoes

- 6 medium sweet potatoes
- 3/4 c. brown sugar
- 1 tsp. salt
- 1 stick margarine
- 1/2 c. milk
- 1 tsp. cinnamon (or pumpkin pie spice)
- 1/2 tsp. grated orange rind
- pineapple slices, maraschino cherries, and tiny marshmallows to garnish

Bake or microwave potatoes until soft. Peel. Put cooked sweet potatoes in a large bowl. Mash with margarine. Add dry ingredients. Add milk, beating by hand or with electric mixer. Put into buttered one-and-one-half-quart casserole. Sprinkle tiny marshmallows on top and garnish with pineapple slices and maraschino cherries. Bake at 325 degrees until heated through and marshmallows are melted.

Yield: serves 4 to 6.

Brennan's Butternuts

- 1 butternut squash
- 2 tsp. butter or margarine
- honey
- ground cinnamon to taste

Cut butternut in half lengthwise. With a spoon, scoop out the seeds and stringy matter. With a fork, pierce the outer skin in several places.

Bake, cut side down, on a cookie sheet covered with foil in a 350-degree oven until squash feels tender when squeezed slightly — 20 to 30 minutes, usually, depending on size of squash. (If you have a microwave, you can cook the squash, cut side down, three minutes at a time, turning after each cooking. Again, depending on the size of the squash this usually takes less than ten minutes.)

Turn squash, cut side up. Place a tsp. of butter or margarine on each half to melt. Drizzle with honey. Sprinkle lightly with cinnamon.

Yield: serves 2.

[*Jim hated squash until he ate something called a butternut. He couldn't believe it was a squash and that he ate the whole thing!*]

Moi Moi (Moyin Moyin)

- 1 c. dried pinto beans or black-eyed peas, ground
- 2 beef bouillon cubes
- 2/3 c. boiling water
- 1/4 c. palm or other vegetable oil
- 1/2 tsp. coarse ground black pepper
- salt
- 6 bay leaves

Grind beans in a coffee grinder, a blender, or a Nigerian *olo*. Mix all ingredients except bay leaves in a bowl. Divide into six portions, placing each portion on a square of heavy duty foil. Top each portion with a fresh bay leaf, and seal the foil packet, making certain to allow plenty of room for expansion. Bake in a moderate, 350 degree, oven for about 55 minutes. Remind guests to remove the bay leaf.

In Nigeria, this dish is wrapped in a native leaf. If the leaf is not available, use foil and a fresh bay leaf.

Yield: serves 6.

— adapted from Juliana Tubi

Kourabiedes (Butter Cookies)

- 1 c. butter
- 1/2 c. sugar
- 2 tbsp. water*
- 1/4 tsp. vanilla extract
- 1 egg yolk
- 2 1/2 c. flour
- 1/2 tsp. baking powder
- 40 whole cloves
- confectioners' sugar
- rose water

Cream butter and sugar until light and fluffy. Beat in the water, vanilla extract, and egg yolk. Sift the dry ingredients together and add to the creamed mixture. Mix well to make a firm dough.

Form rounded tablespoonfuls of the mixture into balls and arrange on a cookie sheet lined with baking parchment. The mixture spreads very little so there is not need to leave big spaces between the cookies. Press each piece of dough lightly with the ball of your thumb to flatten it in the middle and spike the center of each cookie with a clove. Bake at 375 degrees for about 20 minutes until a light golden color.

Transfer the cookies to a wire rack, and while they are still piping hot sprinkle them twice with confectioners' sugar and rose water. When they are completely cold, store in an airtight container.

Yield: about 40 cookies.

* *If desired, use brandy instead of the water.*

Springerle (Aniseed Cookies)

- 4 eggs
- 2 c. sugar
- 1 tsp. powdered aniseed
- 4 1/2 c. flour
- 1 tsp. baking soda

In a large bowl, beat the eggs until fluffy and then beat in the sugar, a little at a time. Continue beating until the mixture falls back on itself in a slowly melting ribbon. Beat in the aniseed.

Mix the dry ingredients and beat them into the egg mixture a little at a time to form a firm dough. Knead the dough on a lightly floured surface until it is smooth and pliable, working in a little more flour if it is too sticky. Chill for about two hours.

On a well-floured surface, roll the dough about 1/2 inch thick. In Germany, the cookies are patterned with a patterned board or rolling pin. If you do not have such a pin, use floured decorative cookie cutters or stamps to make a design on the cookies and cut into 1 1/2" squares. Arrange on cookie sheets lined with baking parchment. Set the prepared cookies aside to dry at room temperature for a day before baking them in a slow oven, 300 degrees, for about 30 minutes. They are cooked when the tops whiten and the bottoms are slightly golden. Cool on a wire rack and store in an airtight container.

Yield: about 40 small cookies.

Speculaas (Spice Cookies)

- 1/3 c. brown sugar
- 1 tbsp. milk
- 1 c. flour
- 1/4 tsp. baking powder
- 1/4 tsp. salt
- 1/2 tsp. cloves
- 1/2 tsp. cinnamon
- 1/4 tsp. ginger
- 1 tbsp. finely chopped almonds
- 1 tbsp. finely chopped candied fruits or raisins
- 5 tbsp. butter or margarine

Put the sugar and milk in a small saucepan and heat gently until the sugar dissolves. Sift together dry ingredients and put in a mixing bowl with the chopped almonds and fruits. Add the dissolved sugar. Cut the butter into small pieces and add, mixing well together. Knead the dough lightly until pliable. Chill well.

To mold the speculaas, dust cookie molds thoroughly with cornstarch before pressing the dough evenly into them. Run a sharp knife along the edges of the design to trim off excess dough, then tap out the molded shapes onto a greased baking sheet. Press large slivers of almond into the design before baking if desired.

Large cookies should be baked at 300 degrees for 45 to 60 minutes. Small cookies bake at 350 degrees for 15 to 30 minutes, depending on size. Cooking is complete when the speculaas are golden brown and firm to touch. Cool on a wire rack and store in an airtight container.

Rovastinpipparkakut

(Bishop's Pepper Cookies)

- 1 egg
- 1 c. sugar
- 1/2 c. dark corn syrup
- 1 c. melted butter or margarine
- 1/4 c. almonds, chopped fine
- 2 1/2 c. flour

- 1 tsp. baking soda
- 1 tsp. cinnamon
- 1 tsp. cardamom
- 1 tsp. ginger
- 1/2 tsp. allspice
- 1/2 tsp. salt

In a large bowl, beat the egg and stir in the sugar, syrup, butter, and almonds. Beat until well-mixed. Sift the dry ingredients together and add, a little at a time, to the syrup mixture, beating until a stiff dough is formed. Chill the dough well.

On a lightly floured surface, roll the dough about 1/4" thick and using plain or fancy cutters stamp out the cookies.

Arrange on well-greased baking sheets and bake for about 10 minutes in a 375-degree oven, until cookies are golden brown and firm to the touch. The exact timing will depend on the size of the cookies. Let them cool a few minutes on the baking sheets before transferring to a wire cooling rack.

Cookies can be iced with a confectioners sugar icing if desired. Let cool and dry completely before storing in an airtight container.

Medeni Kurabii (Honey Cookies)

- 1/2 c. butter or margarine
- 6 tbsp. honey
- 1/3 c. sugar
- 1 tsp. baking soda
- 1 egg yolk
- 1 c. flour
- 4 oz. cube or cake sugar

Melt the butter and mix with honey, sugar, soda, and egg yolk. Gradually add the flour and mix well to make a firm dough. On a well-floured surface, roll rounded teaspoonfuls of the mixture into balls. Coarsely crush the lump sugar and dip the top of each ball of dough into it. Arrange the balls on a cookie sheet lined with baking parchment and bake for about 12 minutes at 350 degrees or until golden brown. Cool on a wire rack and store in an airtight container.

Yield: 2 dozen.

Buche de Noël (Yule Log Cake)

- 1 c. flour
- 1 1/4 tsp. baking powder
- 1/4 tsp. salt
- 1 tbsp. cocoa powder
- 4 eggs
- 2/3 c. sugar
- 1 tbsp. hot water

Sift dry ingredients together. Put eggs and sugar into a large bowl over a pan of hot water and whisk together until pale and thick. Remove bowl from the heat and fold in the flour, half at a time. Add 1 tbsp. hot water and mix lightly. Pour the batter into a shallow pan 13" x 9", lined with baking parchment. Bake at 425 degrees for about 10 minutes.

Turn cake out on a sheet of wax paper cut to the size of the baking tin. Remove the baking parchment and trim the cakes crusty edges. While it is still hot, roll up the cake with the wax paper inside, cover, and set aside until cool.

Assemble with filling on the next page.

Buche de Noël **Filling**:

- 1/2 c. butter or margarine
- 2 1/4 c. confectioners sugar
- 2 tbsp. cocoa powder
- 2-3 tbsp. brandy or rum

Cream together the butter and confectioners' sugar. Blend in the cocoa and liquor, and beat the mixture until it is light and fluffy.

To assemble the cake, unroll the cake and discard the paper. Spread one side with about one fourth of the filling and roll it up neatly. Spread the remaining butter cream over the log. Using a fork, make a ridged pattern like tree bark on the top and sides of the log and circular swirls on the ends like tree rings. Leave the log plain or decorate it with powdered-sugar snow and a sprig of holly.

Makara

- 1 stick margarine, melted
- 1 c. sugar
- 3 eggs
- 2 c. flour
- 3/4 tsp. salt
- 2 tsp. baking powder
- 1 c. buttermilk
- 1 tsp. vanilla
- 1 tsp. ground cinnamon
- 1/2 tsp. ground allspice
- 1/4 tsp. ground clove
- 1/4 tsp. ground ginger

Mix margarine and sugar. Add eggs, one at a time, beating after each. Mix all dry ingredients together in a bowl. Add dry ingredients and milk alternately. Spoon into oiled muffin tins. Bake at 425 degrees for 12 minutes or until top springs back when touched and a toothpick inserted in the middle comes out clean. Makes 3 doz. tiny cakes or 1 1/2 doz. medium cakes. If you like, make a glaze of confectioners sugar and orange juice to drizzle on top, and decorate with chopped fruits or nuts.

— Fred Goporo

Rum Balls

- 2 boxes vanilla wafers, crushed
- 1/2 c. honey
- 4 c. chopped nuts, walnuts or pecans
- 1/3 c. brandy
- 1/3 c. rum

Mix all ingredients together and roll into one-inch balls. Roll each ball in granulated sugar. Store in tightly closed containers, layered with waxed paper. Good after two weeks, better after a month of storage.

Yield: 6 dozen.

— Verna Burke

Kulkuls

- 3/4 c. flour
- 1 tsp. baking powder
- 1/4 tsp. salt
- 1 1/4 c. angel flake coconut
- 1/3 c. melted butter
- oil to fry
- confectioners sugar

Mix all ingredients to form stiff dough. Roll into "snakes" about 1/2 inch thick. Cut into one inch pieces. Fry in hot oil until golden brown.

Make a thin icing of confectioners sugar and water. Pour over pastries in a bowl. Drain and dry on wire racks.

Yield: 3 dozen.

— adapted from Rev. Z. Pazheparampil, S.J.

Struffoli

- 3 c. flour
- 3 eggs
- 1 c. honey, warmed
- pinch of salt
- olive or vegetable oil to fry
- colored candy sprinkles

Sift flour into a bowl. Make a well in the middle of the bowl and add eggs and salt. Mix to a smooth dough. Knead thoroughly and let stand about 1 hour.

Roll dough into ropes about 1/2" thick. Cut pieces about 1/4" long. Fry in hot oil until golden brown. Drain on paper towel.

Place the struffoli in a bowl and pour warm honey over, stirring until all pieces are coated. If you wish, sprinkle colored candy sprinkles over top.

— Rose Rotondi

Mincemeat Pie

- 1 9-oz. package condensed mincemeat
- 1 recipe pastry (see Vennie's Dough, page 162)
- sugar
- brandy

Cook mincemeat according to package directions.

Roll out pastry to cut out tops for individual pies. Fold up trimmings and roll again for rounds to line individual patty tins.

Fill the individual tins generously with mincemeat mixture. Put about a tsp. brandy on top of each filled pie. Cover pie with top crust, dampening edges with cold water and pressing to seal. Sprinkle tops with sugar and bake in hot oven, 400 degrees, for 10 to 15 minutes.

Yield: 1 regular pie or 4 individual pies.

Plum Pudding

- 1 c. fruit bits (1 pkg. Sunmaid dried, mixed fruit)
- 1 c. raisins (yellow, black, or both)
- 1/3 c. chopped candied citrus peel
- 1/3 c. blanched almonds, chopped
- 3/4 c. crumbled bread (1 slice torn in tiny pieces)
- 3 tbsp. flour
- 3 heaping tsp. ground spices (use pumpkin pie spice, or mix your own: cinnamon, allspice, nutmeg, clove and ginger)
- 1 egg
- 1/2 c. butter
- 1 tbsp. honey
- 2 tbsp. brown sugar
- 1/3 c. cognac

Put dry ingredients (first seven) in a large bowl. Stir to mix. In a small bowl put egg, melted butter, honey, sugar, and cognac. Beat slightly until sugar is dissolved and egg is well mixed. Pour over dry ingredients, mixing well.

Generously butter a three-quart metal bowl. Pack ingredients into it. Cover top of bowl with waxed paper and then foil, sealing tightly around the edges. Place bowl in steamer and steam for at least two and a half hours. Cool before unmolding. This pudding will keep a long time if kept in an airtight tin.

I do not have a commercial steamer. Thus I put my flat-- bottomed colander upside down in the bottom of my largest pan. I put the pudding bowl on top of the colander and filled with water about halfway up the side of the pudding bowl. Cover tightly with lid as shown in diagram. Check the water level every half hour to make certain not to boil it all away. All the "traditional" recipes I found only instructed me to use a "pudding basin." My friend Heather who was raised in England told me these were usually ceramic and quite decorative. My cousin Helen tells me that my Aunt Grace made plum pudding each East Texas Christmas in the tins saved from baking soda! I used one of my stainless steel cooking bowls.

The most traditional way to serve the pudding would be to decorate it with a sprig of holly and pour warm brandy over it and light it just as it is brought to table.

Yield: 1 medium pudding.

Chrusciki (Angel Wing Cookies)

- 5 egg yolks
- 5 tbsp. powdered sugar
- 5 tbsp. rum
- 5 tbsp. sour cream
- 1/2 tsp. vanilla extract
- 2 1/2 c. flour plus flour to roll

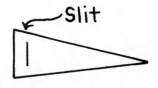

Beat egg yolks well. Add sugar, rum, the other ingredients, and then the flour, gradually. Chill dough for at least one hour. Roll out like a pie crust about 1/8" thick. Cut in thin triangles about 4" long. Put a slip in the wide end and pull the thin end through. Fry in deep fat and sprinkle with powdered sugar.

— Mary Bednarz

Christmas Pudding

- 7 oz. butter or margarine
- 12 oz. currents, washed and dried
- 8 oz. raisins, washed and dried
- 8 oz. sultanas, washed and dried
- 2 oz. mixed, cut peel
- 1 oz. blanched almonds, chopped
- 6 tbsp. rounded, flour
- 1 1/2 tsp. nutmeg
- 1 tsp. ginger
- 2 tsp. cinnamon
- 1 tsp. clove
- 12 tbsp. bread crumbs
- 7 tbsp. brown sugar
- 2 eggs beaten
- rind and juice of one lemon
- 1 tbsp. molasses
- 4 tbsp. beer or milk
- 2 tbsp. brandy (optional)

Grease one large (two-pint) or two medium-sized pudding basins. Melt butter and pour in large bowl. Add the other ingredients and mix well. Put mix in basin and cover top securely with foil. Place in steamer and cover tightly. Steam over fast-boiling water about six hours for a large pudding and four hours for the smaller ones, taking care to add more boiling water as needed.

Cool the puddings and recover with fresh paper. Store in a cool, dry place. The puddings should optimally be made at least a month in advance for the flavour to mature. Steam again for two or three hours before serving. Serve with custard or brandy sauce.

Yield: 1 large or 2 medium puddings.

— adapted from Leo Knowles

Banana *Halwa*

- 2 large ripe plantains
- 2 c. sugar
- 1/4 tsp. powdered cardamom
- 1 tbsp. margarine
- 1 tsp. oil

Peel and cut the plantains into three-inch sections. Place in a steamer basket and steam for seven minutes. Cool and mash with a potato masher. Measure the pulp and add an equal amount of sugar. Put pulp-and-sugar mixture, margarine, and oil into a medium skillet and cook over medium heat, stirring constantly. Cook until a small amount of the mix dropped in cold water can be formed into a solid ball that will keep its shape. Add the cardamom. When the candy is done, it will begin to stick to the bottom of the skillet. Spread the candy on a foil-covered board or a cookie sheet to cool, and cut into pieces when cool.

Yield: 4 dozen 1-inch squares.

— adapted from Rev. Z. Pazheparampil, S.J.

Sugarplums

- 3 c. chopped dried and/or sugared fruit
- 1 c. chopped nuts
- 1 tsp. powdered spice
- 1 tbsp grated orange rind
- lemon juice or brandy
- confectioners or granulated sugar
- plain or colored foil cut into 3" squares

Combine the first four ingredients. Add just enough liquid to enable mixture to stick together. Shape into tiny balls, one to 1/2 inches in diameter. Roll in sugar. Wrap in foil and hang on tree or give as small treats.

Vary the ingredients to suit your own taste and budget.

Suggested fruits are: dates, figs, raisins, candied citron, candied peel, glaceed cherries, sugared dried fruits.

Suggested spice: ginger or cinnamon.

Suggested nuts: any easily available.

The original sugarplums were made in Portugal from fresh fruit cooked for days in ever-thickening sugar syrup. The treat was made most popular in England.

Candied Fruit Peel

- Peels from grapefruit and/or oranges
- powdered ginger (optional)
- sugar
- water

Peel fruit, scraping pulp away from skin but leaving the white underskin. Cut peel into long strips about 1/4 to 1/2" wide. Blanch in boiling water for about five minutes, pour off the water, and repeat three times.

Make a syrup by boiling two parts sugar to one part water. Add powdered ginger to taste. Add peel and simmer gently, partially covered, for about 40 minutes or until peels have absorbed most of the liquid and are tender. After about 30 minutes, check frequently to make certain candy does not burn.

Turn out peels onto a sheet of waxed paper, dredging with the remaining syrup. Let dry for about 24 hours before storing in airtight container. Peel may be used in cooking or eaten as candy.

Snapdragon

- 1 c. brandy, more as needed
- 1 handful blanched almonds
- 1 handful seedless raisins

This game is played most effectively in a darkened room. Place the fruit and nuts in the center of a heavy china platter. Heat the brandy, pour over the fruit and ignite. Guests must snatch the raisins and almonds one at a time from between the flames. Other dried fruits may be substituted for the raisins if you prefer.

Chestnuts have a sacred connotation. They are eaten in Tuscany on St. Simon's Day and on the Feast of St. Martin, when they are distributed to the poor. In Christian symbolism they denote chastity.

The Easter Season

Food plays an important part in the fast and feast of Lent and Easter, helping to enliven and emphasize this most holy of Christian seasons.

Carnival

In ancient times, the law of abstinence was much stricter and included many other foods besides meat. Since medieval times, in many parts of the world, carnival celebrations have been held to anticipate with "one last fling" the coming privations of Lent. The very word carnival comes from the Latin words for withdrawal from meat. On Fat Tuesday (*Mardi Gras* in French), the carnival revelers ate the last of the rich foods, which could not be eaten, nor even kept in the homes, during Lent.

In pre-communist days in the country regions of Russia, carnival was known as "butter week," and a fantastic figure called *Masslianitsa* was gaily decorated and driven about on a sledge while the peasants sang special songs. At the end of the week, this butter goddess was burned, and a formal farewell was bidden to pleasure until Easter. During the week, rich but unsweetened pancakes called *blini* were served in every household. Depending on the topping, these buckwheat pancakes could make an entire meal in themselves.

Despite more than half a century of official atheism, the Russian people still kept their traditions in mind. Easter had long ceased to figure in official calendars, but every year at Easter time the bakeries filled up with traditional baked goods, and even though they were called spring cake, everyone knew them for the Easter sweet they were.

The best known celebration of carnival in America is the famous Mardi Gras in New Orleans — although Galveston, Texas, and several other Southern cities host these celebrations. Parties, parades, masks, and revels are the order of the day. A special cake made in New Orleans is called a king's cake. People serve the cake at private parties. The guest who receives the slice containing a tiny figure of a baby, perhaps Baby Jesus, is the one who will host the party the next year.

In Latin countries, one of the best loved traditions of fiestas and carnivals are the *cascarones*. These are eggshells filled with confetti. Laughing party-goers crack the shells over one anothers' heads for good luck.

Pancakes, known in Italy as *crespelle*, are always eaten on Shrove Tuesday because they are rich, using up the last eggs, butter, and cream before Lent.

Lent

After the feasting and reveling of the carnival season, Ash Wednesday ushers in Lent, the season of penance and fasting, in imitation of Jesus' fast in the desert. Lenten meals in all Christian countries were traditionally meager and simple. Many of these dishes, however, are perfect foods for today's health-conscious lifestyle.

Surprising as it seems, today's popular snack food, the pretzel, has great historical and spiritual significance. In the early centuries of Christianity, this humble snack was a Lenten bread. The faithful in the old Roman Empire kept a very strict fast all through Lent — no dairy products, eggs, or meat were allowed. They made small breads of water, flour, and salt to accompany their simple meals of fish, fruit, and vegetables. To remind themselves that Lent was a time of prayer, they shaped the breads in the form of arms crossed in prayer. The Latin word *bracellae*, "little arms", eventually became the Germanic "pretzel."

The pretzel was the first recreational (therefore junk) food to be widely deplored in this country. Its reputation suffered less for its content than from its frivolous braided shapes, unsuited to the family table. It suffered further, of course, on account of its German origins — at a time when immigration to these shores was not popular with already established Americans — and beer; the German immigrants congregated together in beer halls. (The Moral Majority of the time had the lowest opinion of beer halls, which sprang up wherever the Germans settled: New York, Chicago, Cincinnati.) Later, of course, the Germans, the beer, and the pretzels made their way out to the ballpark, where they all gained a certain cachet in association with sportsmanship and the open air (Chalmers, p. 32).

In the New World, Lenten fasts were never as strict as the old

Grapes were among the first cultivated crops planted by the Franciscan and Jesuit fathers in New Spain, and almost all of the Rio Grande valley was planted to vineyards by the middle of the 1800s. Our predecessors drank more often than we do; wine and brandy were on the table at breakfast, lunch, and dinner (Dent, p. 369).

European ones. Eggs and dairy products were not prohibited, but rather used in place of the forbidden meat. For many Mexican-American families, Lenten memories include special shrimp, egg, and cheese dishes. Some favorites are *albóndigas de camarón* (egg and shrimp fritters), *sopa de pan* or *capirotada* (bread pudding), and *nopalitos* (prickly pear cactus soufflé). For many families, gathering and preparing the *nopales*, or cactus pads, was a family event. The families would go out into the South Texas countryside among the chaparral and mesquite to collect the prickly pear pads, so plentiful in March and April. When enough were gathered, the family sat and talked, keeping a watchful eye out for rattlesnakes, while removing the thorns with paring knives to prepare the fleshy pads for inclusion in a number of regal food dishes.

In England, a charming tradition developed toward the end of the Middle Ages. On the fourth Sunday of Lent, boys and girls who lived as servants away from home were allowed to return to the church of their baptism — their mother church. They then visited their mothers; hence the name Mothering Sunday. Each visitor presented his "mum" with flowers and simnel (plum) cakes and cleaned her house for her.

Wednesday of the fourth week in Lent was called "Middle Cross Day" in the Greek Church, and little cakes baked in the form of a cross were eaten on this day.

In Latin countries, especially Spain and South America, the Feast of the Seven Sorrows was a great day of popular devotions, with thousands thronging the churches to visit the shrines of the Sorrowful Mother. Called the Friday of Sorrows in central Europe, the day was commemorated with a special soup consisting of seven bitter herbs called *Siebenkrautersuppe*. Traditional herbs used were watercress, parsley, leek, nettle, sour clover, primrose, and spinach.

Although we know the day as Palm Sunday in America, this day has various names in other parts of the world. The names come from the plants used. In most countries of Europe, real palms were unobtainable, so people used many other plants in their place. It was customary to bless not only branches but also various flowers of the season. The day was called *Pascua Florida* (flower Sunday) in Spain. The name originally meant just Palm Sunday but later was applied to the whole festive season of Easter Week. Thus, the state of Florida received its name on Easter Sunday of 1513, when

Ponce de León first sighted the land and named it in honor of the great feast.

In central Europe, large clusters of plants interwoven with flowers and adorned with ribbons were fastened to the top of a wooden stick. These palm bouquets were used in the Palm Sunday services and later saved at home behind the door throughout the year. In the Latin countries and in the U.S., the palm leaves are often shaped and woven into little crosses or other symbolic designs which are attached to a crucifix or holy picture, or hung on the wall.

In some parts of Mexico and other sections of South America, it was the custom to reenact the last supper in the church on the Thursday before Easter, with the pastor presiding and twelve men or boys dressed as apostles speaking the dialogue of the Gospels. Afterwards, the faithful made the visit of the Seven Houses, stopping at seven churches, in each of which they receive from the priests a miniature bread in remembrance of the last supper. The faithful, on their part, deposit a coin in each basket containing the bits of bread, in order that it should never be lacking (Quintana, p. 182).

In Malta, a "Last Supper Table" is richly laden by the faithful with food which is later distributed to the poor. In France, children are told that on this day the church bells fly to Rome to fetch the Easter eggs they will drop into each house where the children are good and well-behaved. The day is known as Green Thursday in central Europe and is a day for eating green things, such as a soup of green herbs, spinach, and various green salads.

Good Friday

There is a great deal of symbolism of the Passion of Christ attached to the *capirotada*, which Mexican-Americans eat on Good Friday. The bread is the body of Christ; the syrup is His blood. The cheese represents the Holy Shroud. The cloves in the syrup are the nails of the cross, and the cinnamon sticks are the wood of the cross.

From medieval times onward, it has been the custom in many places to mark a new loaf of bread with the sign of the cross before cutting it. Sometimes, the cross was imprinted on the loaf either by indentation or with sugar frosting. St. Alban's Abbey in England is said to have originated the hot cross buns which became a famous Good Friday feature in England and Ireland and later in the New World. In the mid-fourteenth century, the monks distributed these buns to the poor on Good Friday in place of the ordinary ones. They are round buns made of a spiced dough with a cross of sugar icing on the top. These buns were said not to mold as did regular bread, and eating them on Good Friday was said to protect the home from fire. They were kept through the year to be used as medicine or to ward off disease, lightning, and shipwreck.

In some parts of Italy, farmers still bring wheat to church on Good Friday to be blessed.

At last Holy Saturday arrives, and there is great activity about the house, especially in central Europe, where the Easter ham and other foods for the great feast are prepared. Eggs are boiled and painted and the whole house is decked with flowers and finery. In the Slavic countries, baskets of food, especially the decorated eggs, are taken to the church to be blessed; in other regions, the priests go from house to house to bless the Easter foods. All who come to visit are presented with a decorated Easter egg. In Russia, after the midnight benediction, the people carried their *paska* (Easter bread) to the priest to be blessed, after which it was taken home and given the place of honor on the Easter breakfast table. Easter was the Russian's great day for gift giving (as is our Christmas celebration). It was as Easter presents for his family that Czar Nicholas had the artist Fabergé create the lovely jeweled eggs that have been so often imitated today.

In Ukraine, the blessing of the traditional Easter foods is called *Sviachenia*. Each of the foods in the basket has a symbolic meaning. The beautiful eggs, *krashanky* and *pysanky*, are symbolic of the tomb from which Christ arose, and hold a special meaning of hope. The *pysanky* are highly decorated with Christian symbols and are exchanged with friends and relatives to show the good wishes given to them. The *krashanky*, or plain colored eggs, will be used to break the fast and the entire family will share one of the eggs as a symbol of family unity.

The meat products are ham, roasted lamb, and sausage. These represent the animals used in sacrifice in the Old Testament and remind us of the sacrifice of Christ. The ham symbolizes freedom from the Old Law, and the lamb, symbolic of Jesus, reminds us of the New Law.

Dairy products for the basket are butter, generally made in the shape of a lamb, and various cheeses. The cheeses are bland and symbolize the moderation Christians should have in all things.

Paska and *Babka* are the Easter breads for the *Sviachenia*. They are symbolic of the "living bread," Christ. The breads are rich both in ingredients and in decoration.

Horseradish was part of the original Passover meal to remind the Jews of the bitterness and harshness of life in Egypt. To Christians, it represents the bitterness of sin. This herb is served with red beets to remind us of the bitterness of the Passion of Christ. Salt, a symbol of fast and self-denial, is added to this dish.

In Ukraine, the heavily laden baskets were brought to the early morning Easter services, and afterwards the families gathered outside to admire them. Each basket would contain a lighted candle symbolizing the radiance of the resurrected Christ. The priest sprinkled the baskets with holy water and blessed each food. Then the people greeted one another with the traditional Easter greeting — "Christ is risen, truly He is risen!" They exchanged hugs, kisses, and *pysanky* before departing to their own homes for the Easter breakfast. When religious freedom was still possible in Ukraine, Easter was celebrated for three days. No work was done, the blessed symbolic food was eaten daily, and memorial services for the dead were held, not in sadness but with joyful anticipation because of the promise of life everlasting.

Today the Ukrainians who live in the United States and Canada have started a new custom, the *Sviachene* dinner, which usually takes place on the Sunday following Easter. Just as the meals at home on Easter represented the unity of the family, these dinners sponsored by the church represent the unity of the parish family. The blessed Easter foods are served and many activities are planned, including auctions of *pysanky* and/or *paska*, contests for *paska*, singing, and dancing (Vaughn, p. 17).

In Italy, bread was often formed into Easter baskets or other fanciful shapes. In earlier times these confections were used as ex-voto offerings, with the egg being the traditional reference to life. The *colomba pasquale* is a traditional Italian sweet bread baked in the form of a dove.

Easter

On Easter Sunday, open house is held in most Christian nations. Relatives, neighbors, and friends visit. Easter eggs and bunnies are the order of the day, and special Easter hams are the main dish at dinner. In central Europe, strangers were welcome at any home to eat their fill at the elaborate Easter table. In the Near East, the Christians spent all of the day after Mass and breakfast in visiting friends. The adults enjoyed conversing, and the children were delighted with their gifts of eggs and sweets.

The Easter lamb, representing Christ with the flag of victory, is the primary symbol of the season, and roast lamb has always been a popular Easter food. For centuries it was the main dish served at Easter at the papal table. Today, however, little figures of a lamb made of butter, pastry, sugar, or cake have been substituted for the meat and are used to form attractive centerpieces. Today the traditional Easter meat is ham. The pig has always been a symbol of good luck among the Indo-Europeans, and the custom of eating its meat on festive occasions has been handed down from pre-Christian times. The Christian countries all seem to have certain traditional Easter foods, some of which are *Sucharki Papieskie* (Papal Wafers) and *mazurki* (honey nut cakes) from Poland; *paska*, a Russian Easter bread made with cottage cheese and raisins; *Osterstollen*, a form of raisin bread popular in Germany and central Europe. In Ireland, people enjoy *"golden bread,"* similar to our French toast. Norwegians have a special Easter beer, *paskelbrygg*, and the Hungarians have an Easter meatloaf made of chopped pork, ham, eggs, bread, and spices.

Catholic families in Albania make a special cake called *perpeq* from eggs, flour, sugar, and vanilla. It is similar to the American angel food cake except richer because the yolks of the egg are used. The *perpeq* is usually prepared on Holy Saturday morning and taken that afternoon to the church to be blessed. It is the first food eaten after Holy Communion at the Easter Vigil. Even during the communist persecution, this tradition was continued. The sturdy Albanian Catholics made their *perpeq* in spite of the fact that they would have been imprisoned if they had been found out. After the churches were destroyed in 1967, the people secretly brought the cakes to priests in hiding for the traditional blessing.

The Easter bunny had its origin in pre-Christian fertility lore and has never had much religious symbolism (except for the legend that the rabbit was bleached as the only animal witness to the Resurrection), although it is cherished in the Easter celebrations of many countries as the legendary producer of Easter eggs for children. This legend arose in the Germanic countries, where he was believed to lay red eggs on Maundy Thursday and eggs of other colors the night before Easter. At the beginning of the last century, the first Easter bunnies made of pastry and sugar became popular there; today they are a favorite for children of many lands.

Our pre-Christian ancestors viewed eggs as a symbol of spring and new life. In Christian times, the egg received a religious interpretation and became a symbol of the Resurrection. Since it had been one of the foods prohibited in Lent, people were joyful to be able to enjoy them on Easter. The faithful from early times painted eggs in gay colors, had them blessed, ate them, and gave them as Easter gifts to friends. Their use developed among the nations of northern Europe and Asia soon after their conversion to Christianity. The Roman ritual had a special blessing for Easter eggs:

"We beseech thee, O Lord, to bestow thy benign blessing upon these eggs to make them a wholesome food for thy faithful who gratefully partake of them in honor of the Resurrection of our Lord Jesus Christ."

In most countries the eggs are stained in plain vegetable dye colors. The Chaldean, Syrian, and Greek Christians present each other with crimson eggs in honor of the blood of Christ. Some Slavic peoples made special patterns of gold and silver. The Poles and Ukrainians are famous for their *krasanki* and *pysanki*; each is a masterpiece of patient labor and exquisite workmanship. These eggs are blessed by the priest and distributed among relatives and friends. They are saved from year to year as symbolic heirlooms.

In Germany and other countries of central Europe, the eggs for cooking Easter foods are not broken but pierced with a needle and the contents blown into a bowl. The empty eggshells are used in various ways. Sometimes the hollow eggs are suspended from shrubs and trees during Easter week, decorated much like a Christmas tree. Armenians decorate them with religious pictures and designs to present to the children as gifts.

Easter Monday

In Italy, the Monday after Easter is known as *Pasquetta*, or little Easter. This holiday is celebrated with a picnic, or with a meal eaten at a trattoria in the country.

Ascension Day

Easter week and the days thereafter are ones of happiness and Christian joy in the life of the risen Lord. Although the Church includes the Feast of Pentecost in the liturgical season of Easter, Ascension Day is actually the feast that terminates the events of the Savior's life on earth. This feast has been celebrated since the earliest Christian times, and by the fourth century had spread throughout the entire Christian world of that time.

It was an old European custom to eat a bird on that day because Christ had "flown" to Heaven. In Western Germany, bakers gave their customers pieces of pastry made in the shapes of various birds.

During the Middle Ages in Rouen, a prisoner was chosen and set free on Ascension day. This was done in honor of St. Romain, who was alleged to have delivered Rouen from a dragon in A.D. 520 with the aid of a criminal under sentence of death for murder. The pardoned prisoner was taken to the saint's shrine for confession and absolution. Then, in a large procession led by the archbishop, the fortunate criminal was taken to Mass and then to an elaborate banquet in the house of the master of the Brotherhood of St. Romain.

A Roman superstition tells that if a fresh egg is placed in a basket with a lit candle on a windowsill on the eve of Ascension Day, the Madonna, who passes over the whole world that night, will bless it. A year later, if the egg is opened, a pure wax will be found within which is said to keep misfortune and sickness away.

Pentecost

Pentecost, with Christmas and Easter, ranks among the great feasts of Christianity. It commemorates the descent of the Holy Spirit and the completion of the work of redemption, the fullness of grace for the Church, and the gift of faith for all nations. Whitsunday, or White Sunday, is the English designation of this feast and refers to the newly baptized, who wore white.

The feast was well established by the third century; by the

seventh century the whole week became a time to be considered festive, and work was forbidden for an entire octave. Gradually the holiday was shortened, and today it is generally celebrated on a single day.

From the earliest centuries, the dove has been used as a symbol of the Holy Spirit. The symbolism was inspired by the Gospel report of Christ's baptism and is still popular today. From medieval times on, in many parts of central and eastern Europe, the people hung artfully carved and painted wooden doves over the dining table as a constant reminder to the family to venerate the Holy Spirit.

In Germany, the Whitsun festival is held seven Sundays after Easter. Old and young take to the country that day for a traditional family outing, the *Pfingstausflug*, to celebrate the spring flowers and the new green on tree and in meadow. Banquets were held, and the people drank special "Pentecost beer."

In England, Pentecost Sunday was a day of horse races, plays, and feasting. Gingerbread was hawked at the English fairs held in the countryside during Whitsun week.

Many Americans of Portuguese descent have a great devotion to the Holy Spirit. Beginning around Pentecost and continuing through the spring and early summer, a number of towns in the California Bay Area host *festas* in honor of the Holy Ghost. These *festas* stem from a time in Portuguese history when the country was in the midst of a large famine. Food could not be brought into the country by sea because the ports were constantly shrouded in heavy fog. The people prayed to the Holy Spirit for help. At last a fleet of ships got led through the fog by a white dove, and landed in Portugal. The ships carried beef, bread and, mint. The people made a *sopas*, or soup, of the beef and spice and poured it over the bread. In tribute for their salvation from starvation, the people paid special homage to the Holy Spirit with elaborate parades, folk dancing, and foods.

The California Portuguese *festas* follow a similar pattern. They usually begin on Saturday night with a dance which includes traditional folk dancing. Here the queens are presented. There are several queens for each *festa* with their retinue. On Sunday morning there is a parade through the streets of the town to the church, where there is a solemn high Mass. Then the people gather for a meal of *sopas*. In most places there is only a nominal charge for

When Columbus first spotted chilies growing wild on Santo Domingo, he continued in the same delusion which had led him to name the aboriginal natives "Indians" and he called chilies "peppers." After all, he thought that he had reached the Indies whose fabled wealth was partially made of black pepper and other spices. Chilies in fact are capsicums and have thousands of variants (Dent, p. 59).

the meals, and no guests are ever refused, whether or not they are able to pay the small token. Most of the food is donated through *promesas* (pledges). Gary Silva of Vacaville recalls that when he and his cousin were in the service in Southeast Asia, his grandfather made a promesa of an entire beef for the *festa* if they came back safely. Both returned, and all in the town enjoyed the meat provided by Gary's grandfather in fulfillment of his promise.

The Catholics in Beijing, China, generally have a rich banquet for each of the four first-class feasts of Easter, Pentecost, Assumption, and Christmas. The Joannes Zheng family generally invited some of their Catholic relatives and friends, including a priest, for a banquet on the eve or the evening of the feast. The priest would offer Mass for the family, giving everyone God's blessing. After Mass, all the guests would join to make *Jiao-zhi*, a form of dumpling filled with meat and vegetables. The filling was already prepared by Mrs. Zheng, and the guests would roll and fill the dumplings in the shape of little boats. The unity and cooperation signified their Christian love for one another. Although *Jiao-zhi* signifies good luck and money for the atheists in China, with the Catholics it is a symbol of a boat filled with God's gifts. After the dumplings are prepared, the group enjoys the feast.

Carnival

King's Bread

- 2 pkgs. Rapidrise yeast
- 1 c. milk
- 2 tbsp. flour
- 6 tbsp. sugar
- 1/2 c. melted butter
- 2 tsp. ground cinnamon
- 1 tsp. allspice
- 1/2 tsp. ginger
- 2 c. flour
- 2 eggs, slightly beaten
- 1 tsp. vanilla
- dash salt
- 1/2 to 1 c. chopped dates, raisins, or mixed fruit bits

In a two-cup measure, put yeast, two tbsp. flour, and two tbsp. sugar. Stir to mix. Add one c. warm milk. (Heat milk to scald and cool slightly or put milk in microwave for 45 seconds.) Stir and let yeast begin to work. In five to ten minutes, yeast will have made the mixture grow to two cups.

Stir with a spoon to cause mixture to go back down to about a cup. Add four more tbsp. sugar. Stir and let rest for a few minutes. Place yeast mix in bowl and add butter, eggs, and vanilla. Mix the dry ingredients together and add to liquid slowly, beating with a spoon after each addition. Add the chopped fruit. Spray the inside of a circular metal Jello mold or a Bundt pan with Pam. Spoon in dough. Bake at 350 degrees for 20 minutes or until a toothpick comes out clean. Turn out on plate immediately. Ice while still warm.

Before icing (see next page), make a slit in bread and insert tiny plastic baby to represent Jesus, or a coin or bean wrapped in foil.

[*Today, most king's cakes are purchased in bakeries, not made at home. Here is a quick bread that can substitute for the more elaborate yeast breads provided by the bakery.*]

King's Bread Icing:

- 1 tbsp. melted butter
- 1 1/2 tbsp. milk
- 1 tsp. vanilla
- powdered sugar

Combine butter, milk and vanilla. Add powdered sugar, stirring constantly, to a thick yet still liquid icing. Ice top of cake, letting some icing drip down the side. Decorate with colored sugar, sprinkles, Mardi Gras coins, and beads.

Yield: Serves 4 to 6.

Blini

- 1 pkg. yeast
- 2 c. lukewarm milk
- 1 1/2 c. flour
- 2 tbsp. sugar
- 3 egg yolks
- 6 tbsp. soft butter or margarine
- Another 1 1/2 c. flour
- 3/4 tsp. salt
- 3 egg whites

Dissolve the yeast in milk. Stir 1 1/2 cups flour and the sugar into the yeast mix. Cover and let rise in a warm place for an hour. Beat three egg yolks with the soft butter and add the rest of the flour and the salt. Beat this mix into the yeast mix. Cover and let rise again for another hour. Whip three egg whites until stiff and fold them into the batter. Let the batter rest for fifteen minutes. Lightly oil a small skillet and bake small pancakes. The blini should be thin. Serve with caviar or a fruit topping.

Legend tells that St. Helena had a vision in which she learned that she could find the true cross in a place where the air was sweet with perfume. She is said to have discovered it in a patch of basil.

Lent

Shrimp Salad

- 1 pkg. Uncle Ben's brown and wild rice mix (mushroom)
- 6 eggs, hardboiled
- 1 3/4 c. celery, chopped
- 1 1/2 c. boiled shrimp, peeled
- 1/2 c. onions, chopped fine
- 1/2 c. dill pickles, chopped fine
- 1/2 c. sour cream
- 1/4 c. mayonnaise
- 1 tsp. lemon pepper
- 1/4 tsp. red pepper
- salt to taste

Cook the rice according to package directions. When cool, add all other ingredients. Refrigerate before serving.

Migas

- 1/2 large onion, chopped
- 10 eggs
- 1/2 c. cold water
- 1/4 tsp. red pepper
- 1/4 tsp. salt
- 1/4 tsp. garlic powder
- 1 tsp. cumin
- 6 corn tortillas, torn into pieces
- 6 oz. Monterey Jack cheese (or cheddar), grated
- oil to cover bottom of skillet

Brown onions in oil on medium heat in large skillet. Add tortillas and cook for a few minutes, stirring constantly, to warm thoroughly. Beat eggs with water and spices. Pour in skillet and cook on low heat, covered, for about ten minutes or until eggs are set. Stir once. Sprinkle cheese on top. Cover and continue cooking until cheese melts.

Traditional Pretzels

- 1 pkg. dry yeast
- 1 1/4 c. warm water
- 1 tsp. salt
- 1 tbsp. sugar
- 4 c. flour
- 1/4 c. melted butter
- 1 beaten egg

Dissolve yeast in water. Add salt and sugar. Blend in flour. Knead dough until smooth. Cut into small pieces. Roil into ropes and twist into pretzel shape. Place on lightly greased cookie sheets. Brush pretzels with beaten egg. Sprinkle with coarse salt if desired. Bake at 375 about 15 minutes.

— Jackie Murphy

Pretzels

- 2 tbsp. honey
- 1 c. warm water
- 1 envelope Rapidrise yeast
- 1 tsp. salt
- 3 c. flour
- 1 egg, beaten
- coarse salt
- sesame seed
- Ms. Dash seasoning

Soften yeast in the warm water. Add the honey and 1 tsp. salt. Blend in the flour. Turn out dough on a lightly floured surface and knead until smooth, about five minutes. Roll the dough into ropes about 18" long and shape into pretzel shapes. Place on lightly greased cookie sheet. Brush with beaten egg. Sprinkle with coarse salt or use sesame seed and Ms. Dash non-salt seasoning. Bake at 425 for 12 to 15 minutes until the pretzels are golden brown.

Yield: 10 to 12.

It was Portuguese monks in Nagasaki who, observing the Lenten fast, gave the Japanese the idea that flowered into tempura. The name is a corruption of Quatros Temperos, the Ember (fast) days (Ortiz, p. 8).

Good Friday

Capirotada (Bread Pudding)

- 5 c. water
- 2 cinnamon sticks
- 1 tsp. whole cloves
- 3 thin slices of onion
- 2 c. sugar
- 1 tbsp. butter or margarine
- 18 slices of stale bread
- 12 slices American cheese
- 1 c. raisins

Boil the first five ingredients together for "tea." Strain out spices. Line a large casserole dish with six slices of bread. Put a piece of cheese on top of each piece of bread. Sprinkle with raisins and add "tea" to soak layer. Continue adding layers — bread, cheese, raisins. Top with bread for last layer and add remaining "tea" to soak thoroughly. Bake at 350 degrees for 25 to 30 minutes, until golden brown. Serve warm or cold.

Hot Cross Buns

- 1 pkg. Rapidrise yeast
- warm water to soften yeast
- 2 tbsp. honey
- 1/2 c. milk
- 1 tsp. cinnamon
- 1/2 tsp. ginger
- 1/2 tsp. allspice
- 2 tbsp. grated orange peel
- 1/2 c. raisins
- 2 c. Bisquick

Soften yeast in a small amount of warm water. Mix all ingredients and turn out on a lightly floured surface, kneading for two or three minutes until dough is elastic and shiny. Shape into six to eight balls and place on a lightly greased cookie sheet, flattening tops slightly. Cut a deep cross on the top of buns with a sharp knife. Cover and let buns rise for about 30 minutes. Bake at 400 for 8 to 10 minutes.

Yield: 6 to 8.

(Most recipes are for yeast buns and take several hours to rise. This is a "hurry-up" recipe for cooks in a hurry.)

Nopalitos (Cactus Pads)

- 2 c. nopalitos (buy fresh in produce dept. or canned. Drain canned ones)
- 2 tbsp. cooking oil
- 2 tbsp. flour
- 2 tsp. salt
- 4 eggs
- 1 tbsp. chili powder
- 1 tsp. cumin
- 1 tsp. garlic powder
- 1/2 c. water

Peel and dice fresh cactus pad (or rinse canned nopalitos). Fresh cactus needs to be boiled for 15 minutes, then rinsed and drained. Canned cactus need only be drained. Heat oil in skillet. Add salt, garlic, and chili powder, stirring constantly. Add nopalitos and simmer on low heat for five minutes. Mix flour and water to make a paste and add to the prickly pear. Beat eggs well and fold into nopalitos. Cook until eggs are cooked. Serve with corn tortillas.

Yield: serves 2 to 4.

Albóndigas de Camarón

(Egg and Shrimp Cakes)

- 4 eggs
- 1 1/2 c. shrimp, boiled and chopped
- 1/4 c. minced onion
- 2 tbsp flour
- 1/4 tsp. black pepper
- 1 tsp. salt
- cooking oil

Beat eggs. Add onion, salt, pepper, and shrimp. Add flour and blend to make a batter. In deep skillet, heat cooking oil. Pour 1/4 c. batter for each cake into hot oil. Fry until golden brown, about 1 minute on each side. Drain on brown paper bag or paper towels.

Yield: 1 dozen.

Baked Egg Squares

- 2 c. grated cheddar cheese
- 1/2 lb. hot pork sausage, browned, crumbled, and drained
- 1 doz. eggs slightly beaten
- 2 jalapeño peppers, chopped fine

Generously butter a large glass baking dish. Cover bottom of dish with the cooked sausage. Sprinkle cheese over bottom of dish. Beat the eggs with salt and pepper to taste. Pour over the sausage and cheese. Sprinkle the jalapeños over mix. Bake at 325 degrees until eggs are set and a knife inserted comes out clean, about 30 minutes. Cut in squares to serve. May be served hot or cold.

Yield: serves 4 to 6.

Siebenkräutersuppe (Seven Sorrows Soup)

- 2 c. water
- 2 chicken bouillon cubes
- 4 c. fresh spinach, washed and torn in tiny pieces
- 2 tbsp. finely chopped onion
- 2 tsp. flour
- 2/3 c. sour cream
- dash salt
- dash pepper
- generous sprig of parsley
- small fresh leaf or sprig of each of the following: oregano coriander, basil, dill, garlic leaf*

Bring water to a boil. Add bouillon cubes; stir to dissolve. Add spinach and onion, salt, pepper, parsley and herbs. In a separate cup, stir the flour into the sour cream. Add some of the hot soup stock and stir, then add the mixture to soup, stirring well. Cook over medium low heat until soup thickens.

Yield: serves 4.

If fresh herbs are not easily available to you, substitute 1 tsp. Ms. Dash table blend.

Easter

Simnel Cake

- 3/4 c. margarine
- 2 c. sugar
- 4 eggs
- 2 c. flour
- 1/2 tsp. salt
- 3/4 c. raisins
- 1 c. candied fruit

Cream margarine and sugar. Add eggs one at a time, beating after each. Sift the salt and flour together and add to creamed mixture, beating well. Sprinkle the fruit and raisins with flour and fold into batter. Grease inside of deep cake tin. Pour in batter and bake at 300 degrees for one hour. Frost with thin confectioner's sugar glaze.

Sprinkle toasted almonds on top if desired.

Yield: 1 cake.

The monasteries were a large factor in the preservation of Spanish cuisine. Three of the largest of these monasteries were located in Estremadura. The library of the Monastary of Alcántara was sacked by Napoleon's troops, but one of his officers found and preserved the file of recipes. The great chef Escoffier said this was the best trophy that France gained from that war.

Paska (Easter Bread)

Basic Dough:

- 8 c. flour
- 2 tbsp. salt
- 1 c. warm water
- 1 tbsp. sugar
- 1/4 pound butter or margarine
- 1/2 c. sugar
- 2 c. milk, boiling point
- 1 cake yeast (1 oz.)
- 3 eggs

Crumble yeast in 1/2 c. lukewarm water and add 1 tbsp. sugar. Set aside for five minutes. Pour boiling milk over sugar and butter; add the rest of the water. Cool to lukewarm. Sift flour into bowl, add salt, eggs, milk mixture and yeast. Knead dough until smooth and elastic. Cover and let rise until double, about two hours, in a warm place.

Cheese Dough:

- 1 cake yeast (1 oz.)
- 1 pound dry cottage cheese
- 1 c. raisins
- 4 egg yolks
- 1 c. sugar
- 1 tsp. salt
- 1 tsp. lemon rind
- 1 tsp. baking powder
- 1/2 c. milk
- 3 c. flour

Crumble yeast in warm milk to which one tbsp. sugar has been added and let stand five minutes. Mix cottage cheese with spoon until smooth. Add raisins and yeast mixture. Add unbeaten egg yolks, remaining sugar, salt, lemon rind, baking powder and flour, and knead well. Set aside, covered, to rise until double, about two hours.

Turn basic dough out on lightly floured board and shape into four parts. Let stand, covered, to rest for about 15 minutes. Take one part of dough and lightly punch around the edge so the center is elevated. Take cheese dough and place around the elevated center, then lightly make an opening in the center. Join edges of center with the outside edges, press carefully so that the cheese dough is completely covered. Place into nine-inch tube pan and let rise for about 30 minutes. Cover dough to prevent drying. Just before placing into oven, brush top with egg yolk. Bake for 10 minutes at 325 degrees; increase temperature to 350 and bake for 40 minutes.

Yield: makes 4 *paskas*.

Symbols Bread

- slices of white bread
- cake color
- milk
- Q-Tips
- toaster

In small cups, mix "paint." Use one tbsp. milk and a drop or two of cake color. Using the q-tips as paint brushes, let children paint Christian symbols such as the Chi Rho, the fish, a cross, etc., on the bread. Toast bread in toaster. The designs will intensify in color and puff up. Serve with honey butter.

(This one is for young children who want to help you cook.)

Honey Butter:

- 2 tbsp. softened margarine or butter
- 2 tbsp. honey

Stir together and refrigerate unused portion.

Red Eggs and Pickled Beets

- 1 can (1 lb.) sliced or whole beets
- 1 tbsp. pickling spice
- 1 c. vinegar
- 1/2 tsp. salt
- 1 tbsp. sugar
- 4 to 6 hard boiled eggs, peeled

Drain the juice from one can of beets into a pan. Boil with pickling spice for a few minutes, until you can smell the spices well. Add vinegar, sugar, and salt. Remove from heat. In a large jar, place the beets and eggs, covering with the juice. Refrigerate overnight before eating.

Yield: serves 4 to 6.

Royal *Mazurek*

- 1 c. margarine
- 6 egg yolks
- 1 c. sugar
- 1/4 c. almonds, chopped fine
- 1 1/2 c. flour
- 1/4 tsp. salt

Cream butter. Sift dry ingredients and add, alternately, one egg yolk and a little flour, until all has been used. Add almonds. Bake in a 17 x 11" pan at 350 degrees for 30 minutes. Cool and cut into squares.

Sucharki Papieskie (Papal Wafers)

- 2/3 c. margarine
- 7 egg yolks
- 1/2 c. sugar
- 1 egg
- 2 c. flour
- 1 tsp. baking soda

Cream margarine, add alternately one egg yolk and one tablespoon sugar, and beat well. Add the whole egg. Add flour and baking soda. Mix well. Roll on a floured board to quarter-inch thickness and cut with round cookie cutter. Bake on well-greased baking sheet at 375 degrees for 12 to 15 minutes.

Kowbasa (Polish: Kielbasa)
(Ukrainian [Polish] Sausage)

- 4 lbs. pork
- 1 lb. ham
- 5 tsp. salt
- 2 tsp. pepper
- 1-2 c. water
- 2-3 cloves garlic, crushed
- sausage casings (check with a local butcher shop)

Soak casings for 15 - 20 minutes. Rinse well with cold water. Grind meat on coarse blade. Mix everything together and stuff into casings. Prick casings with a needle to let the air escape. Smoke or bake the sausages.

To bake, place sausages in a pan with a rack; fill with water almost to top of sausages. Bake for 1 to 1 1/2 hrs. at 350 degrees, basting frequently.

Yield: serves 8 to 10.

Heavenly Ham

- 1/2 smoked picnic ham
- 3 tbsp. grape jelly
- 2 tbsp. prepared mustard
- 3 tbsp. dried chopped onions
- 1 small jar maraschino cherries, drained
- 1 small can sliced water chestnuts, drained
- 6 oz. Coca Cola or cola drink

Place ham in large roasting pan without rack, fat side up. Heavily score across the fat in a criss-cross pattern. Stir together above ingredients excepts cherries and chestnuts. This will be a thin sauce with lumps of grape jelly. Stir until the lumps are fairly small. Pour glaze all over ham. Stick cherries and chestnuts into scoring on ham. Place remainder of cherries, chestnuts, and glaze in bottom of pan. Cook according to the timing for the size of your ham. Check frequently to see if there is enough liquid in pan. Spoon juice across top of ham each time you check. If necessary to add more liquid, add cola in small amounts. After slicing ham, spoon water chestnuts and cherries onto platter.

Easter Egg Cheese

- 1 1/2 c. milk
- 6 eggs
- 1 tsp. salt

Beat eggs thoroughly and add milk. Cook in double boiler slowly until mixture curdles and separates into curds and a thin liquid. Pour mixture into a large cloth or a jelly bag and drain off the thin liquid. Squeeze into a large ball, tying the cloth or bag at the top tightly to hold the shape. Hang overnight or until dry. Remove the cheese and cut in slices to serve.

This recipe may be doubled for a larger cheese. For a sweet cheese, add 3 Tbsp. sugar and 1/2 tsp. vanilla to milk and egg mixture before cooking. Cut salt to 1/2 tsp.

This cheese may be eaten plain or buttered and fried or baked (moderate oven for 15 minutes) for variety.

Yield: small (4-inch diameter) cheese.

Easter Monday

Gingerbread

Beat together the margarine, sugar, honey, and 1/2 tsp. soda.

- 1/4 c. margarine (1/2 stick)
- 1/4 c. sugar
- 1/2 c. honey (or use molasses if you have it)
- 1 egg, beaten slightly
- 1/2 tsp. soda
- 3/4 c. boiling water
- 1/4 tsp. soda
- 1 1/4 c. flour
- 1 tsp. baking powder
- 1 tsp. ground ginger
- 1/2 tsp. salt
- 1 1/2 tsp. ground allspice

Add the egg. Sift together spices, flour, and baking powder. Add 1/4 tsp. soda to boiling water. Add the boiling water mix alternately with the dry ingredients, mixing well. The batter seems very thin before it is baked. Pour into a greased, floured pan, 7" X 11". Bake at 325 for 20 to 25 minutes, until middle springs back when touched and a toothpick is clean after insertion in the middle.

Pentecost

Kapusniak (Sauerkraut Soup)

- 1/2 lb. boneless pork shoulder, cut into small cubes
- 4 tbsp. bacon drippings
- 2 medium onions
- 1 carrot
- 2 celery stalks
- 1 parsnip
- 1 lb. sauerkraut
- 3 c. water or stock
- 1/2 lb. smoked sausage
- 1/2 tsp caraway seed
- 1/2 tsp. dill seed
- 1 clove garlic
- 3 tbsp. flour
- 8 small red potatoes
- 1 cup cooked and crumbled bacon

Heat two tbsp. bacon drippings in a heavy frying pan and brown pork, turning often. Add chopped onion, carrot, celery, and parsnip. Cover and cook over very low heat for one hour or until meat is almost tender. Rinse sauerkraut in cold water and chop coarsely. Add to meat and cover with water or stock. Cut sausage into small pieces and add. Add seasonings and cook 30 minutes.

Heat two tbsp. bacon drippings, add flour and brown lightly. Mix in a little broth, and add mixture to soup, stirring and cooking until soup thickens. Scrub potatoes. Cook covered in water for 10 minutes or until tender. Pour off water. Fry bacon crisp and sprinkle over potatoes, tossing lightly.

Serve soup with one or two potatoes in each bowl.

Yield: serves 4 to 8.

— Sister Helena Paskevich, S.S.M.S.

Jiao-zhi

- egg roll wrappers
- 4 chicken bouillon cubes
- 1 1/2 qts. water
- 4 chicken breasts
- 1/4 head cabbage, chopped fine
- 1 small onion, chopped fine
- 1 tsp. ginger
- 1 tbsp. sesame or peanut oil
- 2 tbsp. soy sauce
- 1/4 tsp. salt

De-bone chicken and chop meat into tiny pieces. Place chicken and all ingredients and spices except bouillon in a skillet over medium heat and cook, stirring constantly, until chicken is done and almost all liquid is absorbed.

Spread egg roll wrappers on counter and cut circles with a biscuit cutter. Put a small amount of filling in the center of each circle. Fold the circles in half, scaling the edges by rubbing a small amount of water with your finger and pinching to seal. Curve up the ends slightly to represent a small boat.

In a large pot, bring water and bouillon cubes to a fast boil. Drop the filled dumplings into water and boil for several minutes. The dumplings will first sink and then rise.

Serve *Jiao-zhi* on a plate with a small amount of stock. Garnish with chopped green onions if desired.

Leftover egg roll wrapper pieces may be cut in pieces and fried in hot oil as a crispy snack.

— adapted from Joannes Zheng

In Mexico, chocolate was the subject of a theological donnybrook. In the late 1600s, the ladies of the land were accustomed to having their chocolate served to them in church. They said it prevented fainting and weakness. When one bishop forbade the practice, the ladies took themselves and their entourages to another church, and the offending clergyman, it was rumored, later died of a cup of poisoned chocolate, thus creating a fearful scandal (Rinzler, p. 7).

Portuguese Sweet Bread

- 2 pkg. dry yeast
- 1/4 c. warm water
- 1 c. milk
- 1 c. sugar
- 1/2 c. butter or margarine
- 1 tsp. salt
- 6 c. flour
- 3 eggs, well beaten
- 1 egg, separated, with each part beaten

Dissolve yeast in water. Scald milk, and pour over sugar, butter, and salt in large bowl. Stir until butter melts. Cool. Stir in about two c. of flour and beat until smooth. Beat in three eggs and yeast mixture, stir in only enough flour to make a soft dough. Knead until dough is very smooth and shiny, about 15 minutes, adding flour as needed. Shape into a ball and place in greased bowl; cover and let rise until doubled, about 2 1/2 hours. Punch down and let rest for 10 minutes. Shape bread into loaves or biscuits and place in greased pan. Let rise in warm place until almost doubled. Brush loaves with beaten egg. Bake at 350 degrees for 20 - 25 minutes until golden brown. Cool on wire racks.

Yield: 2 loaves.

— May Martin

Holidays and Holy Days

January 1
New Year's Day
Feast of the Circumcision
St. Basil the Great
Solemnity of Mary, Mother of God

New Year's Day was observed as the Feast of the Circumcision of our Lord since the fourth century. This is also the feast day of St. Basil the Great (now celebrated on January 2). After the major calendar revision of 1970, the Church recognized the day as the Solemnity of Mary, Mother of God.

In Denmark there was a curious New Year's Eve custom. Throughout the year, each household saved its old broken crockery and when New Year's came, the crockery was thrown against the door of favorite friends. The people would dash the crockery against the door and run, but not too far, for when the homeowner came to the door the dasher was invited in for doughnuts. When New Year's morning arrived, the most loved citizens in the community were those who had the most broken crockery before the door.

The Armenians in Persia rose early on New Year's day to make dough. Traditional round cakes full of raisins and almonds were made. A piece of money was baked in one of the cakes, and the person who received it was called the Lord of the Year and was supposed to have good luck all year. After morning Mass, the young men went to the home of the priest to bid him a Happy New Year. He blessed them and gave them something to eat. Together, the priest and the young men went to the homes of other church officers and were again fed. The entire day was spent visiting from house to house. The women also spent the day visiting but went by themselves and not with the men.

In France, *Buche de Noël* (or Christmas log cake) is served on New Year's Eve as well as on Christmas Eve. The number of the New Year is written on the log with decorative icing. The same cake is popular in northern Italy, where it is called *Ceppo di Natale* (Sheraton, p. 63).

In Greece there were two New Year cakes. The first, *vasiloppita*, was a plain yeast-raised brioche flavored with fresh citrus peel and aniseed. This cake was made on New Year's Eve, and a gold coin was inserted after baking. The Cypriot version included blanched almonds. At midnight, the cake was cut with much ceremony. The eldest member of the family divided the cake by the number present plus three. An extra portion was reserved for Christ, one for the stranger or visitor, and one for St. Vassilios (St. Basil). Leftovers were given to the poor on the following day. The gold coin, of course, brought luck to the finder. The second New Year's treat is *melomacarona*, small spiced honey cakes.

December 31 is celebrated in Germany and Central Europe as St. Sylvester's Eve. Flaming punches enhanced the anything-goes free-for-all between the hours of midnight and one A.M. In Italy, lentils are eaten because their shape suggests coins, which is somewhat ironic because lentils (and beans) are generally thought of as a poor people's staple.

In Lebanon, it is said that on the day of the circumcision the trees kneel in prayer for the Holy Infant. Lebanese Catholics serve a special cruller known as a *zalabee* or an *awwamaat*. Yogurt is one of the main ingredients for the light batter of these, which is fried until golden brown and crisp. The crullers are served drenched in a sugar syrup flavored with rose water or orangeflower water.

Melomacarona (Spiced Honey Cakes)

- 2 c. flour
- 1/2 c. olive oil
- 1/2 c. honey
- 1/4 c. sugar
- 1/4 c. brandy
- 1 small orange
- 1/2 tsp. cinnamon
- 1/4 tsp. cloves
- 1 tsp. baking powder

In a large bowl, beat the flour and olive oil until creamy. Add honey, sugar, and brandy. Grate the rind of the orange and then add the juice. Add the spices and baking powder. Beat together into a stiff dough.

Roll heaping tablespoons of the dough into balls, flatten them a little, and arrange well-spaced on cookie sheets covered with baking parchment. With a fork, mark a rigid cross on each. Bake in preheated 350-degree oven for about 20 minutes or until the cakes are a deep golden brown.

Slide the baking parchment and cakes onto a wire cooling rack and let them cool about five minutes before gently easing them off the paper.

Syrup

- 1/2 c. honey
- 1/4 c. water
- 1 tbsp. lemon juice
- sesame seeds or chopped walnuts

Boil honey, water and lemon juice for about five minutes. Cool to lukewarm. Dip the cakes in the honey and arrange on a serving plate. Pour remaining honey over cakes and sprinkle with sesame seeds or finely chopped walnuts.

Yield: 18 cakes.

Zalabee

- 2 c. flour
- 1 pkg. quick rise yeast
- lukewarm water to dissolve yeast
- 1/2 c. lukewarm water
- 1/2 c. plain yogurt
- 1 tsp. salt
- 1 tbsp. oil

Dissolve the yeast in small amount of water. Mix all ingredients, adding more water to make a soft dough. Cover and let set for half an hour to rise. Roll out dough on floured surface and cut into strips. Twist. Fry in skillet of hot oil until golden brown. Drain on brown paper bag or paper towel. Sprinkle with granulated sugar or drench with mint syrup.

Mint Syrup:

Boil together one c. sugar, one c. water and a handful of fresh mint leaves, crushed, until light syrup is formed. Add 1 drop of green cake color if desired. Cool.

January 6
Epiphany
Twelfth Night
Three Kings Day

In many parts of the world, this is the day for gift giving — a tradition carried on from the gifts the "kings" presented to the Christ Child. Kings' cakes are popular in almost all parts of Europe and in many parts of the rest of the world. In almost all countries, these cakes are similar to our coffee cakes, with fruits, nuts, and other toppings being the variation. The cakes are generally made in a round shape or in a ring, and the decorations are often to symbolize the crowns of the kings.

In Brazil, *Dia de Reis* (Day of the Kings) vies with Christmas in the distribution of gifts, especially to children. Children leave their shoes outside the doors expecting gifts from the Wise Men.

In France, a large celebration takes place on the *Fête des Rois*, the Feast of the Kings or Twelfth Night. An elaborate dinner is staged, either in a restaurant or at home (most people prefer to go out for this meal). The main food is a cake in which a bean in hidden. The cake is cut into as many pieces as there are persons in the party. When a man finds the bean he shouts, "The king drinks!" All join in the toast, and he is automatically made the king of Twelfth Night. He then chooses a queen. If a woman finds the bean, the same occurs, and she is crowned Queen of Twelfth Night and picks a king. The king and queen then direct members of the party to follow ridiculous wishes (Hottes, p. 236).

Epiphany is a family holiday for the French, and even the servants return to their homes for a family reunion on that night. After the French Revolution, when even the slightest reference to royalty was anathema to the populace, these cakes were called *Gateaux d'Égalité* (Cakes of Equality), and their religious significance was ignored (Sheraton, p. 34).

In both Greece and Bulgaria, after Mass on Twelfth Day, the priests and congregation used to go to the nearest pool or river. The priest threw a wooden or metal cross into the water to symbolize the baptism of Christ. Young men dived into the water to retrieve the cross, and the one who retrieved it became the hero of the day (Hottes, p. 242).

Italian children receive their gifts from Befana on this day. Befana was an old lady who hesitated to follow the Wise Men, and now she is repentant and takes gifts to all children hoping one day to find which one is our Lord.

In Mexico, the person who gets the bean or the doll (representing the Christ Child) in his slice of the kings' cake will be the one to give a party on Candlemas Day. Throughout Mexico, almost every family puts a kings' cake on the table on January 6, accompanying it with coffee, chocolate, *atoles* flavored with fruits, and salty or sugar *tamales*.

Puerto Ricans hold this day as the principal feast of the season. Baked yams, stuffed banana leaves, and chicken help the people sustain long hours of dancing and singing.

In Rumania, the priest goes to each home to bless it. He dips a bunch of basil in the holy water and uses it to sprinkle the house. The householder gives him a coin and presents him with a bunch of hemp, a ham, and some grain. The priest throws the cross into the water as in Greece and Bulgaria.

In Syria, a special Mass is said, and good wishes and presents are exchanged. Children go from door to door with New Year greetings, and they receive candy and money in return.

A special chocolate candy called Balthazars is made in parts of Eastern Europe. The confection is named for the dark-skinned Balthazar, the Ethiopian Wise Man who tradition says brought the gift of myrrh to the Christ Child.

In the United States, kings' cakes are a popular food for carnival as well as epiphany. They are sold throughout the carnival season with the last day being Fat Tuesday. In New Orleans, a tiny baby is usually baked in the cake, and the person who receives the baby in his slice must give a party the following year. These cakes are rarely baked at home but are a special feature of bakeries in towns which have elaborate Mardi Gras celebrations. In addition to the baby inside, the cake is decorated with carnival coins and beads on top.

Atole

- 1 1/2 c. water
- 1/2 c. *masa harina* (flour paste)
- 2 1/2 c. milk
- 1 tbsp. cornstarch
- 2 cinnamon sticks
- 3/4 c. sugar
- 6 fresh strawberries (optional)

Dissolve the *masa harina* in one cup of water. Strain through cheesecloth, and put in a medium saucepan. Add remaining water, milk, cornstarch, cinnamon, and sugar. Cook over medium heat, stirring occasionally, until mixture is the consistency of heavy cream. If too thick, add milk. Cut each strawberry in fourths and add to serving cups.

Batatas (Baked Yams)

- 3 lbs. yams
- 1 c. milk
- 1/2 c. butter
- salt
- black pepper
- pineapple slices (optional)
- maraschino cherries (optional)

Peel the yams and cut into thin slices about 1/4" thick. Sprinkle lightly with salt and pepper. Butter a shallow casserole dish and arrange the slices of yam in overlapping layers, dotting each layer with small pieces of butter. Pour in the milk. Garnish the top of dish with sliced pineapple and maraschino cherries, if desired. Bake, uncovered, for about 1 1/2 hours or until the yams are tender.

Yield: serves 6 to 8.

January 17
St. Anthony, Abbot

St. Anthony, a holy abbot who died in 356, is known as the father of monasticism. Although he lived to be 105, legend reports that he had to endure severe temptations and that the devil often appeared to him in the form of a pig. Pork is the traditional fare of the dinner on St. Anthony's feast day (Kaufman, p. 96).

Ham Salad Spread

- 1 can deviled ham
- 2 green onions, chopped fine, including stems
- 1 small dill pickle, chopped fine
- 1 tbsp. dill pickle juice
- 2 hard-cooked eggs, chopped into small pieces
- 2/3 c. mayonnaise
- 1/2 tsp. garlic powder

Mix all above ingredients. Refrigerate 30 minutes. Spread on bread for sandwiches, or use as a dip for chips.

— Ora Bolton

January 19
St. Canute IV

On the feast of St. Canute, the Danes honor a great king and martyr. At Christmas, a cake baked in the form of a boar is brought to the dining room table, but it is not eaten until St. Canute's Day, January 19, when the Danish Christmas Season ends.

Ham Tarts

- 3/4 c. margarine
- 1 1/2 tsp. prepared mustard
- 3 c. ground cooked ham
- 3/4 c. green pepper, finely chopped
- 2 tbsp. minced onion

Soften margarine. Mix with mustard. Stir in remainder of ingredients. Fill 48 tiny tart shells. Bake at 450 for five to six minutes.

Yield: 48 small tarts.

— Verna Burke

January 21
St. Agnes

St. Agnes is unquestionably one of the most famous of the Roman martyrs. The name of this youthful third-century virgin martyr means lamb or victim in Latin, and pure in Greek. A basilica was first built in her honor about the year 350. For centuries, two lambs have annually been blessed on the altar of the Basilica where her relics lie. They are sent to a cloister where they are reared. From their wool come the palliums sent by the Pope to archbishops who wear them on their shoulders as symbols of the sheep carried by the Good Shepherd.

A lamb cake is a nice remembrance on St. Agnes's feast. This is baked in a lamb-shaped mold, frosted white and made woolly with coconut shreds. Raisins serve for eyes and a half cherry for the mouth.

St. Agnes Lamb Puffs

- 1 egg
- 1/2 c. beer
- 3 tbsp. sugar
- 1/4 c. sesame seed
- 2 1/2 c. Bisquick
- oil to fry
- confectioner's sugar

In a bowl, slightly beat the eggs with the beer and sugar.

Add the Bisquick, stirring to mix thoroughly. Turn out on a heavily floured board and roll to quarter-inch thickness. Sprinkle both sides with sesame seed; roll across with rolling pin to sink seed into dough. Cut out puffs with lamb-shaped cookie cutter. Put about one inch of oil in a small skillet and fry puffs in hot oil, one or two at a time. Drain on paper and sprinkle with powdered sugar.

Yield: 1 dozen.

There is a story that mole sauce, so popular in Mexico, was created by the nuns in a convent in the Mexican city of Puebla. The dish was to be served to a visiting bishop for Sunday dinner, and was originally made with turkey, a native bird. The peppery flavored sauce was conventionally Mexican, but at the last minute the cook grated in some bitter chocolate.

February 1
St. Brigid

St. Brigid, the "Mary of the Gael," is, except for St. Patrick, Ireland's favorite saint. Although ascertainable facts of her life are few, her legend abounds with acts of charity, often including the multiplication of food. In Ireland, a spiced yeast bread called barm brack is baked for her feast, and neighbors are invited to join with the family in an evening of feasting and fun in her honor.

St. Brigid's Bread

- 2/3 c. butter or margarine
- 1/3 c. sour milk
- 1/4 c. brown sugar, packed
- 1/2 c. granulated sugar
- 1 pkg. yeast
- 1 egg
- 1 c. oats
- 1 c. Bisquick
- 2 tsp. cinnamon
- 1 tsp. allspice
- 1/2 tsp. ginger

Heat butter and milk to melt butter in microwave (or melt butter and scald milk). Add sugars. Allow to cool slightly and add yeast, stirring to mix. Let mixture rest for 10 minutes. Add slightly beaten egg. Mix all dry ingredients and stir into yeast mix. Lightly grease a pyrex pie plate. Pour in batter and bake at 375 degrees for 20 to 25 minutes. When done, allow to cool slightly and serve warm with butter.

February 3
St. Blaise

St. Blaise is the patron saint for diseases of the throat, and on his feast day crossed candles are used to bless throats. Blaise, a fourth-century Armenian bishop and martyr, while he was in prison, cured a young boy who had a fish bone stuck in his throat. His relics were brought to Italy in 732 by Christians fleeing persecution in Asia Minor.

In Rome, in the church bearing his name, a choral Mass according to the Armenian rite is said on his feast, after which small loaves of bread are given out. Hard biscuits such as *mostaccioli* are traditionally eaten on the saint's feast.

In central Europe and in the Latin Countries, people are still given blessed breads — *Pan bendito* — of which they eat a small piece whenever they have a sore throat.

Blaise Biscuits

- 1 egg
- 1/2 c. beer
- 1 tbsp. sugar
- 2 1/2 c. Bisquick

In a bowl, slightly beat the eggs with the beer and sugar. Add the Bisquick, stirring to mix thoroughly. Turn out on a heavily floured board and roll to half-inch thickness. Spray a glass pie plate with oil and place biscuits touching sides. Bake at 375 degrees for about 15 minutes.

Yield: 1 dozen.

(*In Europe, hard biscuits are served in honor of St. Blaise. Here we have soft, fluffy, light biscuits named in honor of this saint.*)

February 5
St. Agatha

In the legend of St. Agatha, her breasts were severed during her martyrdom. This story is honored on her feast by bread baked in round loaves. In the region near her birthplace of Catania in Sicily, little rounded marzipan confections meant to simulate breasts are also eaten on her day as special treats. Catanese nuns make the sweets which are called *minne de vergine*. The legend has led to her veneration today as a patroness in cases of breast cancer.

According to legend, Agatha miraculously freed her native city from starvation and stopped an eruption of the volcano Etna. Therefore, she is venerated as a "bread" saint and a patron against fire. On her feast day, people baked "Agatha loaves," to which they attached little pieces of paper with her picture and handwritten prayers against fire. The loaves were blessed in church and kept as a sacramental.

St. Agatha's Gold (Hot Cheese Fingers)

- 1 glass Old English cheese
- 1 stick margarine
- 1 beaten egg
- 12 slices of bread, crust removed and cut in half

Mix margarine, cheese, and egg, beating to form a smooth icing. Ice top and sides of bread slices. Bake on an ungreased cookie sheet at 350 degrees for 5 to 10 minutes. Serve hot. These can be made in advance and refrigerated until used.

Yield: 12 double fingers or 24 singles.

— Helen Nixon

February 14
St. Valentine

The legend of St. Valentine tells of a young priest who lived in Rome in the third century. He was jailed for refusing to renounce his Christian faith. In prison, Valentine sent letters to his loved ones via a dove that came and sat on his cell window. The message simply said, "Remember your Valentine."

Valentine, along with St. Marius and his family, assisted the martyrs who suffered during the reign of Claudius II. According to his "acts," after his arrest the Prefect of Rome first imprisoned him, then had him beaten with clubs and beheaded. While in prison, he restored sight to the little blind daughter of his judge, Asterius, who thereupon was converted with all his family and suffered martyrdom with the saint. The date of his martyrdom is thought to be about 270.

The pagan Romans celebrated Lupercalia, a great feast, on February 15. On the eve of the feast, and as part of it, the young people held a celebration of their own, declaring their love for each other, proposing marriage, or choosing partners for the following year. The couples sometimes exchanged presents. The Roman youth festival was under the patronage of the goddess Juno Februata. After the Roman Empire became Christian, the feast was changed to the patronage of the saint whose feast was celebrated on February 14, the priest and martyr Valentine.

In the 17th century, a hopeful maiden ate a hard-boiled egg and pinned five bay leaves to her pillow before going to sleep on Valentine's Eve, believing this would make her dream of her future husband.

To this day, St. Valentine is honored as a patron for lovers and sweethearts. For Catholics, he remains a symbol not only of our love for one another, but of the love between God and man.

Red Velvet Valentine's Cake

- 1/2 c. shortening
- 1 1/2 c. sugar
- 2 eggs
- 1 tsp. vanilla
- 1 tsp. butter flavor
- 3 tbsp. cocoa
- 1 oz. red food color
- 2 1/2 c. cake flour
- 1 c. buttermilk
- 1 tsp. salt
- 1 tbsp. vinegar
- 1 tsp. soda

Cream shortening, sugar, eggs, and flavors. Make a paste of cocoa and food coloring. Add to first mixture. Alternately add flour and buttermilk. Mix soda and vinegar in small bowl. Add to batter. Blend. Pour into three nine-inch greased cake pans, preferably heart-shaped. Bake at 350 degrees for 20 to 25 minutes. Frost when cool.

Frosting:

- 3 tbsp. flour
- 1/2 tsp. salt
- 1 c. milk
- 1 c. shortening
- 1 c. sugar
- 2 tsp. vanilla
- 1/4 tsp. butter flavor

Cook milk, flour, and salt until very thick, about the consistency of cooled pudding, stirring constantly. Let cool thoroughly. Cream shortening and sugar, adding flavors. Combine with the first mixture. Beat well. Frost between layers and on top, letting icing drip down sides.

The uneven texture of this light, buttery frosting evokes the idea of antique lace over the red velvet cake. Or frost with any plain white icing of your choice.

— Verna Burke

March 17
St. Patrick

St. Patrick, the great apostle and patron of Ireland, died in 461. His cultus developed early, and he was greatly venerated from early times. Today, the popular celebration on St. Patrick's Day in the United States consists of traditional details. In the morning, families attend Mass. Then there is a solemn parade, with subsequent meetings, speeches, festive meals in the home, and entertainment in the evening.

Potato dishes have been a traditional part of St. Patrick's Day dinner since the time of suppression of the Irish Catholics by the English.

Rev. Kevin Shanley, O. Carm., is the son of Irish immigrant parents. St. Patrick's Day was both a holy day and a holiday. After attending the parade, the family had a festive meal. Irish Soda Bread was served as a reminder of the family's ancestral roots in Ireland. This bread was usually served as a dessert to top off a meal which often featured Irish potatoes and sometimes corned beef and cabbage.

Irish Soda Bread

• 3 c. flour
• 2/3 c. sugar
• 1 tbsp. baking powder
• 1 tsp. baking soda
• 1 tsp. salt
• 1 1/2 c. raisins
• 1 3/4 to 2 c. buttermilk
• 2 eggs, lightly beaten
• 2 tbsp. melted shortening

Combine dry ingredients in a large bowl. Add buttermilk, eggs, and shortening to make a soft dough. Add raisins and knead a few minutes on a lightly floured surface. Form a round loaf about two inches thick. Place on a lightly floured or mealed baking sheet; cut a cross on top. Bake at 350 degrees for about an hour.

Yield: 1 loaf.

— Rev. Kevin Shanley, O. Carm.

Best Boiled Potatoes

- 20 small red potatoes
- garlic salt
- dried parsley flakes

- 1 stick margarine
- 1 c. milk

Boil potatoes until tender (test with fork). Drain off water and fork open potatoes. Add margarine and milk. Sprinkle liberally with garlic salt and parsley flakes. Stir to coat all potatoes.

Yield: serves 3 to 5.

Irish Coffee

- 1/2 pint whipping cream
- 4 tsp. sugar
- 1/2 tsp. vanilla

- Irish whiskey
- coffee

Whip the cream with sugar and vanilla. Place in the refrigerator to chill. Make full-strength coffee. Pour into six cups or mugs, stirring 1 tsp. sugar into each. In each cup pour one jigger of Irish whiskey. Top with whipped cream and serve immediately. Canned dairy topping can be substituted for the whipped cream.

Yield: 6 cups.

March 19
St. Joseph

Joseph, the husband of our Lady, earthly father of our Lord, guardian of the Holy Family, is honored liturgically on March 19 as patron of the Universal Church and again on May 1 as patron of workmen. This quiet, just man is loved by many nations. A symbol of humility, protector of families, he is honored as patron of fathers, the poor, and craftsmen. He is invoked as a helper for a happy death.

In Italy, Joseph is one of the most loved saints. On the eve of his feast, it was once a custom to light bonfires in the middle of the town square in his honor. In some parts of the country, after the noonday Mass, a banchetto was held on his feast day. A large table, "*tavola di San Giuseppe*," was set on the piazza, or town square. The table was covered in white and decorated with flowers. Townspeople brought the best of their dishes. A man, woman, and child, representing the Holy Family, were led in solemn procession to a decorated platform where they were seated as guests of honor. Then all enjoyed the sumptuous banquet. The poor, especially, loved the day, for they were allowed to take the remains home with them. After the banquet, the people sang and danced around the bonfires until late in the night (McLaughlin, p. 99).

In Sicily, from the time of the Middle Ages, a special altar was made on the saint's feast day. A great famine had seized the island, and the starving farmers implored the aid of St. Joseph. Their prayers were answered, and in gratitude they offered their most valuable possessions, their food, to the saint.

This tradition is carried on today by many Americans of Sicilian descent. The beautiful altars have become elaborately decorated feasts for the eye as well as for the palate. In Sicily, the altars were erected in family homes, usually in thanksgiving for favors granted. Those less fortunate were invited to join the feast. In America, the immigrants did not know their neighbors as well and began making their altars in more public places such as churches and halls.

The feast begins with the ceremony of the saints. Children are chosen to represent the Holy family, favorite saints, and angels. Twice they knock on doors, seeking shelter, and are turned away. At last, they knock and are warmly welcomed with the words, "What I have is yours. Come and sit at my table." They are then reverently served.

In New Orleans, Jesus opens the ceremony by cutting the bread. St. Joseph is always served first, and tradition denotes the order in which the courses are presented. Except for the pasta, there are three portions of the same food on each plate to symbolize the Trinity and the Holy Family. The feast begins with fruit, and follows with bread, pasta, seafood, vegetables, cookies, desserts, and water and wine. *"Mangiate, santos dolces"* ("Eat, sweet saints"), says the moderator before each course. At the close of the ceremony, the saints are given one of the symbolic breads. Then the guests are invited to partake of the meal (Moore, p. 5).

In Galveston, Texas, the Knights of Columbus annually host a beautiful altar which is an outgrowth of a private one originally built many years ago in thanksgiving for St. Joseph's aid. The wood from the original altar is still used each year. In their ceremony, a special Mass begins the feast. Then the ceremony of the saints is enacted. All who wish may attend; there is no charge, although a basket for donations is usually well filled. After the delicious feast. the beautiful and decorative breads and cakes and the flowers from the altar are auctioned. Money raised is given to the poor.

Each St. Joseph's altar has a uniqueness of its own, due to the different cooks who prepare it. There are also similarities. Although these altars are generally large, we have made a miniature for our home in the spring. The altars generally have three tiers to symbolize the Blessed Trinity.

A statue of St. Joseph and a statue or picture of the Holy Family are placed on the top tier and decorated with flowers, greenery, and fruit. The altar is blessed by the priest, usually in a special ceremony, before anything is removed from it. If the altar is set up on the eve of the feast, people often visit to pray and to leave petitions and donations for the poor.

At the house where the altar is erected, a fresh green branch is often placed over the door to indicate that the public is invited to share the food.

The beautiful breads are baked in symbolic shapes. This bread may be eaten, but pieces are saved by the devout. Through the year in case of a storm a small piece is thrown out, and St. Joseph's aid is invoked to protect the household. Keeping a piece of this blessed bread with you is said to insure against a violent death, and many of our Italian-American friends keep pieces of the bread in their car and in their homes. When I attended my first St. Joseph's altar, I jokingly asked if the bread didn't mold (ours is a very damp climate). One of our friends, looking a bit startled at my question, thought about it a minute and then assured me that St. Joseph wouldn't mind moldy bread. Interestingly enough, the piece of bread which I brought home and put on our family altar dried out thoroughly but has never turned moldy.

Some of the symbols often pictured on the St. Joseph's altar are the monstrance, chalice, cross, dove, lamb, Bible, hearts, wreath, palms, lilies, sandals, beard of St. Joseph, ladder, and tools. A braided loaf symbolizes the staff of St. Joseph, which according to legend bloomed with entwined blossoms to single him out from among all Mary's suitors as her spouse-to-be. Other traditional foods are also found on the altars. *Mudica* is a type of seasoned bread crumb for the pasta which represents the sawdust of Joseph the carpenter. *Pignolatti* are fried pastries in the shape of pine cones. Legend tells that the Child Jesus played with pine cones for toys as a child. *Pupaculova* is a baked bread filled with dyed Easter eggs symbolizing the coming of Easter. Wine reminds the participants of the wedding feast of Cana. In addition to other fruits, there are generally grapes, olives and figs because these are grown abundantly in Sicily.

Guests at the altar are invited to take home fruit and sometimes other small objects which have been placed on the altar, such as holy cards, medals, and fava beans. The blessed beans are in remembrance of a time when the beans, originally grown only for animal fodder, grew in abundance when the other crops failed. In desperation, the farmers ate the beans and were surprised at their good taste. It became known as a "lucky bean." Legend has it that the person who carries a blessed bean will never be without coins. It can also be a sacramental to remind us to pray.

[*When Michael found out I was writing a Catholic cookbook, he suggested I include his favorite dish in honor of his patron St. Joseph. When I asked what it was he replied, "Untidy St. Joseph." I am afraid I looked a little askance until he explained: "You know, sloppy Joe!"*]

Charlemagne, the ruler who united most of the people of Europe into a single Christian community around the year 800, gave his empire not only peace and good government but also advice on how to plant herb gardens and vineyards and directions on the amounts of food to be used at every meal (Hazelton, The Cooking of Germany, p. 90).

Untidy St. Joseph

- 1 lb. ground beef
- 1 c. catsup
- 1/4 c. water
- 1 tbsp. barbecue seasoning*
- 1/2 tsp. garlic powder
- hamburger buns

Cook and crumble the ground beef in a skillet. Spoon off excess fat. Pour in catsup and water. Add spices and stir until mixture is heated through. Serve on hamburger buns.

Yield: serves 4 to 6.

*If your store does not sell pre-mixed barbecue seasoning, make up a batch for your spice shelf from the following:

- 3 parts paprika
- 2 parts celery seed, ground
- 2 parts coriander seed, ground
- 1 part black pepper
- 1 part nutmeg, ground
- 1 part salt
- 1 part red pepper, ground
- 1 part chili powder
- 1 part onion powder
- 3 parts garlic powder
- 1/2 part cloves, ground

Pasta e Fagioli

- 2 tbsp. butter or margarine
- 3 tbsp. onions
- 2 c. water
- 1 8-oz. can tomato sauce
- 1 16-oz. can chick peas
- 1 tsp. oregano
- 1 clove garlic
- 1 tsp. basil
- salt and pepper to taste
- 1 8-oz. package fettucini

In a large saucepan, melt butter and saute onions until transparent. Add all other ingredients except pasta. Bring to a slow boil, reduce heat, and simmer. Cook pasta according to package directions until almost done. Drain and add to pot. Simmer another five minutes.

Yield: serves 4.

— Joan Neubauer

Pane

- 2 pkg. active dry yeast
- 2 1/4 c. lukewarm water
- 10 c. flour, sifted
- 2 tsp. salt
- 1/4 c. oil
- 1 egg yolk mixed with 1 tbsp water
- sprig of mint
- sesame seeds

Sprinkle yeast over water to soften. Place flour in a large bowl, make a well in the center and add the yeast mixture and salt. Stir to combine. Knead about 10 minutes or until dough is smooth. Pour oil over dough and continue to knead until dough is no longer sticky, about five minutes. Cover dough and let rise in a warm place until doubled in size.

Test dough by pressing with the fingertip. If your finger leaves an indentation which remains, the dough is ready. Shape into two loaves or symbolic shapes and place in greased baking pans. cover and let rise in a warm place until doubled. Brush the tops of the loaves with the egg mixture using a mint sprig. Sprinkle with sesame seeds. Bake in preheated 425-degree oven for 10 minutes. Reduce heat to 375 and continue to bake until golden brown or until loaves sound hollow when tapped, usually about 30 minutes. Cool on a rack.

— Elizabeth Moore

Pignolatti

- 2 c. flour
- 1/4 tsp. salt
- 3 eggs
- 1/2 tsp. vanilla
- oil for frying
- 1 c. sugar
- 1/2 c. honey
- 2 tbsp. margarine

Combine flour and salt in a large bowl. Make a well in the center. Combine eggs and vanilla; add to flour mixture. Mix well to make a stiff dough. On a lightly floured surface, knead dough 10 to 12 times. Roll dough to a 12 x 7-inch rectangle. Cut dough into strips 1/4 inch wide and 1/2 inch long. Roll each strip into a small ball. Heat oil in a deep saucepan and drop as many pieces of dough as will float. Fry dough for two to three minutes, or until golden.

Drain on paper toweling.

In a heavy skillet, combine the sugar and honey. Cook and stir over medium heat until sugar is dissolved and mixture boils. Cook an additional three minutes, stirring occasionally. Stir in margarine. Pour over deep-fried pastries in a large bowl. Stir to coat well. Working quickly with buttered hands, form the coated pieces into cone-shaped mounds.

— Elizabeth Moore

Pupacoulova

- 2 c. flour
- 2 tsp. baking powder
- 1/2 tsp. salt
- 1 c. sugar
- 3/4 c. vegetable shortening
- ice water
- 6 eggs, raw and colored

Mix dry ingredients and work in the shortening until crumbly. Add ice water until it forms a dough. Roll out on a floured surface and cut into circles (about three inches in diameter). Line muffin cups with the dough rounds, pressing gently with fingers to fit cup. Put a dyed egg into each basket and decorate the tops of the eggs with dough that has been cut into flowers. Cut 12 three-inch strips from dough. Twist together and shape to form basket handles. Bake handles on cookie sheet and egg baskets in a preheated 350-degree oven until done. These will not get very brown. Attach handles to baskets after baking, using white Karo syrup.

Yield: 6 baskets.

— Elizabeth Moore

St. Joseph's *Sfinge* (Cream Puffs)

- 1/2 c. butter or margarine
- 1 c. hot water
- 1 c. sifted flour
- 1/2 tsp. salt
- 4 eggs
- 1 tbsp. sugar
- 1 tbsp. lemon rind, grated
- 1 tbsp. orange rind, grated

In a saucepan, mix water, sugar, butter, and salt and bring to a boil. Add flour, beating vigorously with a wooden spoon until mixture leaves sides of pan and forms a smooth ball, then continue cooking and stirring about three minutes. Remove from heat and quickly beat in the eggs, one at a time, beating until smooth. Continue beating until mixture is smooth and glossy. Add the grated rind, mixing thoroughly. Drop by tablespoonfuls two inches apart on a lightly greased baking sheet. Bake at 450 for 15 minutes. Lower heat to 350 and continue baking for another 15 to 20 minutes or until golden in color. Remove to a cake rack to cool completely. Cut a slit in side of each puff and fill with French Vanilla Cream Filling, or fill with whipped cream, vanilla pudding, or a ricotta cheese filling.

Yield: about 16 puffs.

— Rose Rotondi

French Vanilla Cream Filling:

- 1/2 c. sugar
- 2 tbsp cornstarch
- 1/4 c. flour
- 1/4 tsp. salt
- 2 slightly beaten egg yolks
- 1/2 c. milk
- 1 c. hot cream
- 1 c. hot milk
- 2 tbsp. butter
- 2 tsp. vanilla

In top of double boiler, blend together first four ingredients. Blend together egg yolks and one half c. milk. Add to the dry ingredients, stirring until smooth. Add hot milk and cream, blending in well. Cook over boiling water, stirring constantly, until thick. Cover and cook for five minutes. Remove from heat and add butter and vanilla. Cover and cool. Fill sfinge.

— Maddi Rotondi

Zeppola di San Giuseppe

- 8 c. flour
- 2 cakes yeast
- 2 1/2 c. lukewarm milk
- 3 eggs
- 1 c. sugar
- grated rind of 1 lemon
- pinch of salt
- 6 tbsp. butter
- oil for frying
- confectioners sugar for icing

Sift flour into a large bowl and make a well in the center. Dissolve the yeast in 1/2 c. lukewarm milk and pour into well. Work it with flour, gradually adding more of the milk until the dough is workable but fairly stiff. Knead until smooth and elastic, then cover bowl and leave the dough in a warm place to rise for about two hours or until doubled in bulk. Punch down dough and work in eggs, beaten with sugar, lemon rind, and salt. Knead until thoroughly blended and smooth again. Melt butter over low heat in about seven tbsp. of milk, cool to lukewarm, and gradually add to dough, kneading vigorously all the time. Dough will be fairly soft and sticky. Continue to knead until it comes away cleanly from fingers.

Sprinkle pastry board lightly with flour and roll dough out about one quarter inch thick with floured rolling pin. Cut into circles about 2 1/2" in diameter. Spread the circles out on a lightly floured cloth and leave them to rise again until doubled in bulk.

When ready to fry doughnuts, heat plenty of oil in a deep pan to 350-360 degrees. Fry doughnuts two or three at a time until puffed and golden brown on both sides. Drain on paper and dust with confectioner's sugar.

— Rose Rotondi

Pasta Milanese

Sauce:

- 3 medium onions, chopped
- 4 cloves garlic, minced
- 4 tbsp. olive oil
- 1 12-oz. can tomato paste
- 1 tbsp. sugar
- 2 to 3 c. water
- 1 18-oz. can tomato puree
- 1 15-oz. can tomato sauce
- 2 2-oz. cans anchovies, chopped
- 1 tsp. oregano
- 1 tbsp. dried basil
- salt and pepper to taste

Saute onion and garlic in olive oil until transparent. Add tomato paste and sugar; simmer about 10 minutes. Gradually add water, tomato puree, tomato sauce, and anchovies. Season with herb. Cover and cook over a slow fire for 1-1/2 to 2 hours.

Pasta:

- 1 tbsp. olive oil
- 1 c. chopped fennel
- 1 1 lb. package vermicelli

Add olive oil, fennel, and vermicelli to rapidly boiling salted water. Cook *al dente*. Top with Milanese sauce and Mudica.

Mudica

- day old hamburger or hotdog buns
- olive oil
- anchovy oil (optional)
- cinnamon
- sugar
- salt and pepper to taste.

Toast buns in a slow oven (300 degrees) until golden brown and crisp. Crush with a rolling pin or blend in a food processor until finely crushed. Saute crumbs, stirring constantly in a small amount of oil until they are a deep amber color. Lightly season with cinnamon, sugar, salt and pepper.

Yield: serves 6 or more.

— Elizabeth Moore

March 25
The Annunciation
(Lady Day)

Two symbols are associated with this feast. The first, the lily, is well known. The second, the stork, Christians have long forgotten to associate with Our Lady. The stork denotes piety and chastity, and it is associated with the Annunciation because as the stork announces the coming of spring, so the annunciation to Mary indicates the coming of Christ. The northern European tradition that newborn babies are carried to their mothers by the stork is a derivation from its association with the Annunciation (McLaughlin, p. 50).

The lily is the flower of the Annunciation. In many Renaissance paintings, the angel Gabriel holds a lily or there is a lily in the picture of the angel and Mary. To carry out the lily theme of this feast day, make lily sandwiches.

Lily Sandwiches

- 9 oz. cream cheese
- 2-4 tbsp. cream or milk
- 20 slices fresh white bread
- 1/4 tsp. salt
- 1/8 tsp. paprika
- green pepper
- carrot

Combine and work into a paste the cheese, cream, salt, and paprika. Remove crusts from bread. Roll into cornucopia shape by bringing two straight edges together and letting them overlap slightly. Hold the edges together with a little cheese, pressing gently. Roll and chill the bread "lilies" before filling. After sandwiches are filled with the cream cheese mixture, insert a thin strip of carrot for a stamen. Cut bell pepper into leaf shapes and attach a leaf to each sandwich with additional cheese. Chill sandwiches until time to serve. Decorate the serving tray with a plastic stork.

Yield: 20 finger sandwiches.

— Helen McLaughlin

April 23
St. George

St. George is listed as a martyr who suffered in Palestine before Constantine. Many legends have grown up about him, although we have little accurate information. One of the most famous legends tells of his slaying a large dragon, and he is almost always pictured in art with this symbol. Since the earliest Christian times, he was revered in the East as patron of soldiers, and he is the patron of England.

In Spain there are many festivals celebrating the liberation of Spain from the Moors, such as the festivals centered around St. George. The festival at Alcoy is the most lavish. A dish credited to Cuba known as *Moros y Cristianos* (Moors and Christians) is popular both in Spain and Latin America. In the dish, black beans are served with white rice.

An ancient Spanish soup which may have originated during the struggle between the Spanish people and their Moorish conquerors is called *gazpacho*. The Spanish guerrillas would have traveled light. In addition to their weapons, they probably only carried wooden bowls and wine skins. Slipping up to a friendly farmhouse, they were given oil, vinegar, onion, garlic, water, bread and probably cucumber from which they made a type of cold soup. After the reconquista, when the Spanish themselves became conquerors, they brought back from the New World and added to their soup tomatoes and sweet green peppers.

Gazpacho

- 1 46-oz. can tomato juice
- 1 tsp. garlic salt
- 2 tbsp. lemon juice concentrate
- 2 tbsp. Worcestershire sauce
- 1 tbsp. sugar
- 2 tbsp. olive oil
- 1/4 tsp. black pepper

- 4 tsp. picante sauce
- 1 can tomatoes, cut, with juice
- 2 c. chopped celery
- 2 c. cucumber, grated
- 2 c. green pepper, chopped fine
- 2 c. grated carrots
- 1 large onion, chopped fine

Mix all ingredients and chill well before serving.
Serve with garlic toast.
Yield: serves 12 to 15.

— Carolyn Kares

Moros y Cristianos

- 1 16-oz. pkg. black turtle beans*
- 1 tsp. dried basil
- 1 bay leaf
- 1/2 tsp. cumin
- 1 medium onion, diced
- 1 clove garlic, minced
- 1/2 tsp. red pepper
- 5 slices uncooked bacon chopped into small bits
- salt to taste
- white rice, cooked according to package directions

Soak beans overnight. Rinse, throwing out those that float. In a large pot, place the bacon bits. Cook over medium heat, stirring constantly, until bacon is partially cooked. Add beans* and enough water to cover about an inch. Add all spices except salt. (Add salt to beans only when cooking is completed; otherwise your beans will be tough.) Bring beans to a rapid boil, then put on low heat. Cook until beans are tender, usually 30 minutes to 1 1/2 hours. Serve over rice.

Yield: serves six to eight.

Black turtle beans are smaller than their oriental cousins and have a tiny white mark on their seam. If you use the oriental black bean, expect a much longer cooking time.

Melachrino Cake (St. George Cake)

- 3/4 c. butter
- 1 2/3 c. sugar
- 3 eggs
- 1/4 tsp. nutmeg
- 1 1/4 tsp. cinnamon
- 1/4 tsp. ground cloves
- 1 1/2 tsp. baking soda
- 1/3 tsp. salt
- 1 2/3 c. flour
- 3/4 c. milk
- 1 1/2 tbsp. lemon juice

Cream the butter and sugar. Beat in three eggs. Sift in spices, soda, and salt with the flour. Add the milk alternately with the dry ingredients. Stir in the lemon juice. Pour the batter into a greased 9 x 14-inch loaf pan. Bake in a moderate oven, 350 degrees, for 45 minutes. Turn out and glaze while warm.

Glaze:

- 2 c. confectioner's sugar
- 5 or 6 tbsp. water
- 1/2 tsp lemon juice

Put the sugar in a bowl and add the juice. Add water until the mixture is the texture of pancake batter. Pour over warm cake.

April 25
St. Mark

April 25 is the feast day of St. Mark the Evangelist, the patron saint of lawyers, glaziers, and the Venetian republic. A traditional rice and pea soup called *risi e bisi* is served on this day in memory of the days when it was ceremoniously offered to the doge of Venice. The peas represent the arrival of spring, and the rice represents abundance.

St. Mark was with Peter in Rome, and according to legend Mark then went on a preaching voyage along the shores of the Adriatic. He later founded the Christian Church in Alexandria, which was the place of his martyrdom. In the ninth century, his relics were brought to Venice.

Salt cod from northern Norway was known as fastenfleisch, or fast-day meat.

Risi e Bisi (Rice and Peas)

- 6 tbsp. margarine
- 3/4 c. chopped onion
- 1 1/2 c. white rice
- 2 c. frozen green peas, thawed
- 4 1/2 c. water

- 4 chicken bouillon cubes
- 1 tbsp. chopped parsley or parsley flakes
- 1/2 c. grated Parmesan cheese
- salt and pepper to taste

Boil the water and add the bouillon cubes to dissolve. In a large skillet, melt the butter and add the onion. Saute until the onions are clear. Add the rice. Cook, stirring constantly, over medium heat, until rice begins to brown. Add the broth and return to boil. Add peas. Cover tightly and reduce heat to low. Cook until rice is tender. Check at 15 minutes. Add the parsley, cheese, and salt and pepper to taste. Serve in bowls.

Yield: serves 6.

June 13
St. Anthony of Padua

Anthony of Padua was a great Franciscan preacher and wonder-worker. Although born a Portuguese aristocrat, he is highly honored by the Italians and is known as the special advocate of the poor. When something is lost, St. Anthony is the one to ask to help find it. Alms given in his name are called "St. Anthony's Bread."

In the early 1900s, St. Anthony's feast was widely celebrated by the Italian Americans in upstate New York, almost surpassing even the county fair for crowds.

St. Anthony is the patron saint of the city of Lisbon, capital of Portugal. Here, the saint's feast is celebrated by everyone eating grilled fresh sardines as well as by the large fiesta in his honor. In some sections of Europe it became the custom to serve liver on the saint's feast, although the origin of the custom is not clear.

Bacon and Liver Bits

- 1 pkg. chicken livers
- sliced bacon
- worcestershire sauce
- 1/2 lemon
- toothpicks

Cut each chicken liver in two or three pieces. Wrap 1/2 strip of bacon around each liver and secure with a toothpick. Place a few drops of worcestershire sauce and a drop or two of lemon juice on each piece.

Broil, turning once, until liver is cooked and bacon is nicely browned.

June 24
St. John the Baptist

Patristic tradition holds that John the Baptist was freed from original sin and sanctified in his mother's womb. From earliest times, therefore, the Church has celebrated his birthday and acclaimed him as herald of the Son of God. (Other saint's feasts are usually celebrated on their death — their birth into Heaven.) The cult of this saint was one of the most important cults in the Church through the Middle Ages, although it has declined somewhat in recent times.

The use of fire and bonfires on the eve of St. John's feast stems from customs of our pre-Christian ancestors. In many parts of medieval Europe, this midsummer feast was celebrated with singing, dancing, and, of course, festive foods. In Normandy at Jumièges, up to the first half of the nineteenth century, the festival was marked by a traditional celebration of the Brotherhood of the Green Wolf. Their chief donned a peculiar costume which consisted of a long green mantle and a very tall green hat and stalked at the head of the brothers, chanting the hymn of St. John. They processed to the parish church for Mass and then adjourned to the house of the Green Wolf, where a simple supper was served.

In Sardinia at the end of March or the first of April, the young men of the villages presented themselves to the young ladies and made a pact to be sweethearts. At the end of May, the girls made pots from the bark of the cork-tree and filled them with earth, sowing wheat and barley in each pot. By St. John's Eve (also known as Midsummer's Eve) the plant had a good head on it. On St. John's Day, the couple dressed in their best and went in procession to the local church where they threw the pot against the door of the church, after which they sat and ate eggs and herbs to the music of flutes. Wine was passed around, and all partook.

In Sicily, couples became "gossips" (sweethearts) of St. John on his feast. They presented each other with plates of sprouting corn, lentils and canary seed which had been planted before the festival.

In Rome, St. John's night is celebrated with the eating of snails.

At Catania, the gossips exchanged pots of basil and great cucumbers. In Portugal, basil and garlic were the important plants in his cult (Ball, p. 133). On the eve of the feast, people danced through the streets until all hours, hitting each other with leeks.

In New York, the many Americans of Puerto Rican descent

honor St. John as patron of Puerto Rico. In the early '60s, thousands of them flocked to the outdoor Mass held on Randall's Island, and to the fiesta that followed. Processions, piñatas, and picnics marked the fun-filled afternoon.

Lazy *Pyrohy*

- 2-3 large onions, sliced
- 2 sticks margarine
- 1 lb. large-curd cottage cheese
- 1 lb. sauerkraut, cooked and drained
- 1 lb. wide noodles, cooked and drained
- 1 lb. sour cream

Fry onions in butter until just barely brown. Pour over cooked noodles and mix well. Add pepper to taste. Add the rest of the ingredients. Mix well. Warm through over a low heat to allow flavors to blend thoroughly.

Yield: serves 4 to 6.

— Sister Helena Paskevich, S.S.M.S.

June 29
St. Peter the Apostle

Simon Peter was a fisherman of Bethsaida when Christ called him, along with his brother Andrew, to be a "fisher of men."

As a fisherman turned fisher of men, St. Peter is often depicted with a fish, and in a number of countries it has been the custom to eat fish on his feast day. In some places, fishermen and fishmongers gave fish to the poor in his honor (Vitz, p. 254).

Spicy Fried Fish

- fresh or frozen fish filets — red snapper or flounder
- 2 eggs
- 1/2 c. beer
- 1 c. flour
- 1 c. yellow corn meal
- 1/2 tsp. lemon pepper
- 2 tsp. paprika
- 1 tsp. garlic powder
- 1/2 tsp cayenne pepper
- 1/2 tsp. onion powder
- 1/2 tsp. salt or to taste
- oil to fry

Beat eggs in a bowl. Add beer and 1/2 c. flour, beating well. Put fish filets in batter.

Mix all dry ingredients with the other half c. flour. Put into a paper or plastic bag. Add filets, one at a time, shaking to coat fish with breading. Fry in hot oil.

Sts. Peter & Paul Mounds

- 1/3 c. mashed potatoes
- 1 3/4 c. powdered sugar
- 2 cans, 4 oz. each, coconut
- 4 oz. semi-sweet chocolate

Mix cool potatoes, sugar and coconut. Shape in mounds and put in refrigerator to chill. Melt chocolate and pour over each piece.

Yield: 18 pieces.

— Verna Burke

July 2
The Visitation

The feast of the Visitation recalls Mary's great humility. The violet is a symbol of humility, and St. Bernard referred to our Lady as the "violet of humility." Candied violets can sometimes be found in gourmet shops or can be homemade.

Candied Violets

- bunch of violets
- 1 egg white

- granulated sugar
- small paintbrush

Pick violets in the early morning. Whip egg white until frothy. Work over a plate of granulated sugar. Using a small paintbrush, coat each violet carefully with the egg white. Sprinkle sugar on violet and lay it on a plate of sugar. Allow to dry. Use to garnish cakes or other desserts, or eat as candy.

August 1
Lammas Day

In Britain, up to the time of the Middle Ages, this day was kept as a day on which thank-offerings were made for the grain crop that had just been harvested, if the harvest was a good one. The people came to church and brought offerings of loaves of bread baked from the new wheat. This is how the day got its name — lammas is a shortening of "loaf Mass" (Harper, p. 199). Although the day is no longer celebrated, it is a precursor of other special days still very much alive — England's modern harvest festival and America's Thanksgiving.

August 2
St. Roch

This fourteenth-century healer was on pilgrimage to Rome when a great plague began. He nursed those afflicted, and when he became ill himself, legend has it that he was nursed back to health by a dog, which is often shown with him in art.

In Calabria, the feast of this saint is celebrated with Italian gingerbread figures called *panpepati*, which represent various parts of the body. These are ex-votos for people whose arms, legs, or various organs are protected by the saint and to whom they offer the baked symbols.

We'll make our gingerbread whole men to celebrate with St. Roch our healthy bodies and whole souls in God's love.

Gingerbread Men

- 1/2 c. shortening
- 1/2 c. firmly packed brown sugar
- 1 egg
- 1/2 c. molasses
- 1 1/2 tsp. vinegar
- 3 c. flour
- 1/2 tsp. soda
- 1/2 tsp. salt
- 1/2 tsp. each ground ginger, allspice, cinnamon
- 1/4 tsp. ground cloves

Cream shortening and sugar. Add egg, beating well. Add molasses and vinegar. Sift together the dry ingredients and stir into wet mix. Chill dough. Roll on lightly floured board to one-eighth-inch thickness. Cut with gingerbread man cutter. Place on greased cookie sheets and use raisins to form features of face and buttons. Bake at 350 degrees for 10 to 12 minutes. Remove at once to cool. Frost if desired with thin confectioners icing.

Yield: 2 or 3 dozen.

August 10
St. Lawrence

St. Lawrence was a Christian deacon who was martyred in 258 in Rome. Although it is most likely that he was beheaded, tradition holds that he was roasted slowly to death on a gridiron. At one point, he supposedly told his tormentors, "Turn me over, for that side is quite cooked enough."

Because he kept the books for the church, Lawrence is the patron of librarians as well as of bakers and cooks.

In Italy, it is the custom not to cook on the feast day of this saint, and to serve only cold foods.

Golden Granola Grabbits

- 3 eggs, beaten slightly
- 1/2 c. brown sugar
- 1/2 c. margarine, melted
- 3 c. rolled oats
- 1 c. coconut flakes
- 1/2 c. blanched and slivered almonds
- 1/2 c. raw cashew nut pieces
- 16 oz. pkg. Del Monte dried fruit bits
- 1/2-1 c. golden raisins

In a large bowl, mix the eggs, brown sugar and margarine. Add the oats and coconut and stir well to moisten all. Add the nuts and stir to coat.

Spread mixture on a lightly oiled standard cookie pan. Bake at 300 degrees for an hour. Check and stir mixture after 30 minutes, breaking into bite-size chunks. Check each 15 minutes thereafter. When mixture is a pleasant golden brown, remove from oven to cool. Immediately on removal, add the fruit and raisins, stirring gently to allow the fruits to stick to the oat-nut clumps.

Store in an airtight container. Eat as a snack or serve with milk as a breakfast cereal.

Cucumber Soup

- 1 large cucumber
- 2 tbsp. chopped green onions
- 1 tsp. salt
- 1 1/2 tsp. powdered mustard

- 1 tsp. garlic powder
- 1 c. sour cream
- 1 qt. buttermilk

Peel cucumber and grate. Add all other ingredients, mixing well. Chill before serving.

August 15
The Assumption

The Assumption is one of the greatest of all the festivals that the Church celebrates in honor of the Mother of Christ. It commemorates her death and assumption into heaven.

Polish Americans honor Mary on this day as Our Lady of the Flowers. Portuguese-Americans held family celebrations and baked a special Portuguese bread which was distributed after the feast.

In Armenia, the blessing of grapes takes place at Mass on this day. These are the first grapes of the season to be eaten. An old custom here dictates that all women named Mary entertain their friends on this day.

In Belgium, as in Armenia, the day has something of the tone of a harvest thanksgiving. Processions go from church to fields and the new fruits and grains are blessed (Harper, p. 207). Italy and Spain held colorful processions, and Italian-American colonies in big American cities often observe the day much the same as they would in their homeland.

One of the strangest celebrations of the Assumption is centered at the monastery near Damascus in Syria. Here people come from far and near bringing offerings of new wheat to the Virgin. What makes this unusual is that Muslims come, too, and join with the Christians in this festival (Harper, p. 209).

In some countries, the Assumption is the day for the blessing of herbs. An old legend held that all the flowers and herbs on earth had lost their scent after Adam and Eve had sinned in the Garden of Eden. On the day of the Assumption, the flowers were given back their scent, and the herbs their power to heal (McLaughlin, p. 66)

In the Byzantine Rite, the Assumption is celebrated as Our Lady's Falling Asleep. On this day, sweet basil and other herbs are blessed and used in seasoning various dishes.

According to tradition, crescent rolls were first produced by the bakers of Vienna, who expressed their rejoicing in the Christian victory over the Turks in 1683 with a roll in the shape of the Muhammadan crescent.

Rose Water

To make rose water, fill a saucepan with well-washed red rose petals and add water to barely cover. Bring to a boil then reduce heat, cover and simmer for five minutes. Cool and strain. Rose water was praised in seventeenth-century herbals as a cordial to revive faint spirits. It was also doused on hot fire shovels to perfume a winter room. In many cuisines, it is used as a mild flavoring, especially in candies and icings. A few drops mixed with glycerine makes a soothing hand-and-body lotion. Refrigerate, as this could mold when kept on the shelf.

Lemon Dill Butter

- 1 tbsp. grated lemon rind
- 3 to 5 sprigs of fresh dill, finely chopped
- 1/4 tsp. salt
- 8 oz. soft butter or margarine

Blend lemon rind, dill, and salt into butter. Refrigerate several hours before serving. Delicious on most green vegetables.

Sweet Basil Butter

- 1 tsp. dried basil leaves, crumbled
- 1 tbsp. sugar
- 8 oz. soft butter or margarine
- 1/4 c. blanched almonds

Whirl almonds in a food processor or chop into small pieces in a coffee grinder. Stir all ingredients into butter or margarine.
Refrigerate several hours before use.

Herb Vinegar

Thoroughly clean bottles with a thin neck and some form of stopper. Worcestershire sauce, soy sauce, and some other condiment bottles are fine. Drop fresh sprigs of herbs into bottle, stem end down. A chopstick will help with the insertion of the herbs. Boil white vinegar. Pour into bottle over herbs. Cap loosely. The following day you may need to add a few drops more of vinegar to fill the bottle as some will be absorbed by the herbs. Some good combinations of herbs are shown, but don't be afraid to experiment with your own combinations. Allow vinegar to stand in a dark place at least a week before using. Mixed with oil, herbed vinegars make a tangy salad dressing, or sprinkle on meat before cooking for flavor and tenderizing effect. Use:

- 1 clove garlic, peeled
- 5 1x1/8" slices of lemon peel
- 3 or 4 sprigs of dill weed
    or
- 1 clove garlic, peeled
- 1 sprig rosemary

- 2 or 3 sprigs of oregano
    or
- 1 small bay leaf
- 2 or 3 sprigs oregano
- 3 to 5 tiny red or green ornamental peppers

All herbs used in the above combinations are easy to grow in most climates. Flavored vinegars make a nice gift from your garden.

August 16
St. Stephen of Hungary

St. Stephen was the first king of Hungary. He worked energetically for the conversion of his people to Christianity. He once was venerated by the universal Church on September 2 because a great victory over the Turks was obtained at Budapest in 1686 through his intercession. Today, his feast is kept on August 16. A festive dinner is part of the traditional observance of his feast in Hungary.

Chicken *Paprikas*

- 1 fryer/broiler, cut into pieces
- 1 tbsp. butter
- 1 tbsp. shortening
- 1 tbsp. paprika
- 1/2 tsp. crushed red pepper
- 1 small onion, chopped
- 1 pint sour cream
- 1 tbsp. flour
- salt to taste

In heavy skillet, melt the butter and shortening. Add onion and cook over low heat until onion turns clear. Add the spices. Add the cut-up chicken, cover, and cook on medium to low heat until well done (about 45 minutes). Stir the flour into the sour cream. Add to chicken and cover. Simmer on low heat for a few minutes, just until gravy thickens slightly.

— adapted from Mary Janovcik

Kolachki

- 1 c. milk, scalded
- 1/2 c. sugar
- 1/2 c. margarine
- 1 pkg. yeast
- 3 eggs, beaten slightly
- 1 tsp. salt
- 5 c. flour

Add sugar and margarine to scalded milk. Cool slightly and add yeast. Let rest for five minutes and add eggs. Pre-measure flour and salt into a bowl. Using an electric mixer, slowly add flour to yeast mixture until dough becomes to thick for mixture. There should be about a cup of flour left. Begin to knead, adding rest of flour as needed. Put dough in bowl, covered, and set in a warm place to double. Turn dough out on a lightly floured board and knead gently until dough is soft, satiny, and elastic. Divide dough into six balls. Roll each ball on lightly floured surface and cut each into 12 squares. Put a small amount of filling in center of each square. Fold corners to center, gathering tips and pinching in middle. Place filled *kolachki* on cookie sheet and allow to rise for 20 minutes before baking. Brush tops of kolachki with a beaten egg mixed with a little milk and sugar. Bake at 350 degrees for 15-20 minutes, or until lightly brown.

Cottage Cheese Filling:

- 1 lb. dry cottage cheese (usually called farmer's cheese; if all available is creamed cottage cheese, place in strainer and allow whey to drip for 30 minutes)
- 1/4 c. sugar
- 1 tbsp. butter
- 1 egg, beaten
- 1/4 tsp. lemon rind
- 1 tsp. vanilla

Melt butter, cool slightly. Add egg, sugar, and cheese. Add lemon rind.

Other fillings: Poppy seed and prune filling (*lakvar*) are available in most grocery stores. Any fruit pie filling is also useful.

Yield: 6 dozen.

August 28
St. Rumbald of Kent

According to his legend, St. Rumbald must have been the shortest-lived saint on record. At his birth, he cried, "I am a Christian," three times and demanded baptism. After baptism, he walked to a nearby well, preached for three days and then died.

Whatever the true facts about this saint, they were so long ago that we cannot determine the basis for this absurd legend. We do know, however, that for several centuries fishermen from Kent invoked the blessing and protection of this saint. From each catch, they saved the eight largest fish and sold them, putting the proceeds in a special fund which accumulated for an entire year. Then on Christmas Eve they spent the entire year's savings on one great feast, which they called a "Rumbald" in honor of their patron. The custom died out long ago, but even now in Kent one sometimes hears Christmas Eve referred to as "Rumbald Night" (Harper, p. 221).

Pink Salmon Fritters

- 1 15-oz. can pink salmon
- 1 beaten egg
- 1/2 c. flour
- pepper to taste
- 1 heaping tsp. baking powder
- 1/2 tsp. Worcestershire sauce
- 1/2 c. chopped green onions
- oil for frying

Drain salmon, reserving juice. Mix salmon and egg with fork. Add flour, pepper, onions, Worcestershire sauce. Add baking powder to quarter c. of the reserved liquid. Add this to the rest just before ready to fry. Drop in deep hot oil from spoon.

Yield: serves 2 to 4.

— Helen Nixon

September 8
The Nativity of the Blessed Virgin Mary

The Nativity of the Virgin is the name day for all girls named Mary. It is the day to have blueberries in some form, especially for breakfast, for the color is symbolic of the Virgin in her blue mantle.

Naturally it is not possible for anyone to have twelve birthdays in one year, but in the Coptic and Abyssinian Churches, the first day of each month is celebrated as the birthday of the Virgin Mary. In addition, they also devote the entire month of May to special honors for Mary as their way of showing how important they consider her.

There are only three birthdays in the Church calendar. The stories of the births of Jesus and John the Baptist are told in detail in the New Testament, but nothing appears there about Mary's. By the end of the seventh century, Christians had established September 8 as her birthday and kept it as a feast.

In Mexico, the people lead up to this day with a week-long fiesta in honor of the "Virgin of the Remedies" (Harper, p. 232).

In France, this is the day of the grape harvest festival. Vineyard owners brought their best grapes to church to have them blessed, and tie some of them to the hands of the statue of the Virgin. Here, the feast is called "Our Lady of the Grape Harvest," and a festive meal is held at which the first grapes of the new harvest are eaten.

In the Alps, the "down driving" began on this day. The animals were brought down from the high mountain slopes to take up their winter quarters in their warm stables. The day is a festive one and ends with a large banquet uniting the family and farm hands in each home. In some parts of the Alps, the milk obtained on this day is given to the poor in honor of Our Lady, along with the leftovers from the feast (Weiser, *The Holyday Book*, p. 113).

Blueberry Cheese Pie

- 1 9" graham cracker pie crust
- 8 oz. pkg. cream cheese
- 1/2 c. sugar
- 1 tbsp. lemon juice
- 1 tsp. vanilla
- pinch salt
- 2 eggs
- 8 oz. sour cream
- 2 tbsp. sugar
- 1 tsp. vanilla
- 2 c. fresh or frozen blueberries
- 1 c. water
- 1 tbsp. cornstarch
- 1 tsp. cinnamon
- 2 tbsp. sugar

Soften cream cheese. Beat in sugar, beating until fluffy. Add lemon juice, vanilla and salt. Add eggs, one at a time, beating after each. Pour into pie shell and bake at 325 until set, about 25 to 30 minutes. Stir sugar and vanilla into sour cream. Spoon on top of pie and bake 10 minutes longer.

In small saucepan, mix water, cornstarch, cinnamon, and sugar. Bring to a boil, stirring to prevent sticking. Mixture will thicken. Add blueberries.

When pie is slightly cooled, spoon cooled blueberry topping over top. Refrigerate.

September 27
Sts. Cosmas and Damian

According to their legend, Cosmas and Damian were twin brothers who practiced medicine without charging fees and were martyred during a persecution of Christians in Syria. They are invoked as patron saints of physicians.

A large *festa* in honor of the twins, known as the *Medici*, was held annually in Utica, New York, at the church of St. Anthony of Padua. The gathering was like a gigantic party, with crowds numbering in the thousands. The festival was brought to Utica at the beginning of the century by immigrants from Bari and Alberobello in southern Italy, where the *Medici* are particularly venerated.

Families went first to the church for special blessings. Then there was a procession, followed by a return home for a huge meal that always began with chicken soup with greens and tiny meatballs. Back at the festival, the people strolled about listening to the various band concerts and sampling pastries from the stands.

Chicken Soup

- 1 whole chicken, cut up (omit organ meat)
- 1 small bunch green onions, chopped, including stems
- 2 c. milk
- 2 c. water
- 6 to 8 medium mushrooms, sliced
- 2 tbsp. cornstarch
- 1 tsp. black pepper
- 1 tbsp. parsley flakes
- 1 small carrot, diced
- 1 small pimento or red bell pepper, diced
- 2 tbsp. margarine
- salt to taste

Bake chicken until done. Cool. Remove all meat from bones. In a large pan, melt the margarine. Dissolve cornstarch in water. Place all ingredients in pan. Bring to a boil and reduce heat to low. Cover and cook 15 to 20 minutes.

Yield: serves 4 to 6.

Hot Sausage Balls

• 1 lb. hot sausage

• 8 oz. sharp cheese, grated

• 3 c. Bisquick

Mix above ingredients. Roll into balls about the size of a large marble. Place on cookie sheet. Bake at 325 degrees for 30 to 45 minutes, until lightly browned.

Yield: 6 dozen.

— Verna Burke

September 29
St. Michael the Archangel

Holy Scripture describes Michael as one of the chief princes (Dan. 10:13), and as the leader of the heavenly armies in their battle against hell (Rev. 73: 7-8).

Waffles baked in a Gaufrette iron are traditional for Michaelmas Day in Italy. The Scots bake St. Michael's Bread (McLaughlin, p. 116).

In Northern Spain, Michael was acclaimed as the national patron of the Basques. Here his feast was kept with great celebration.

In the north of Europe and in England, wine consumed on St. Michael's feast was called Saint Michael's Love.

Whatever you eat on this day, however, pass up the blackberries! The devil put his foot on them the night before, and every blackberry in the world is poisoned. Why this superstition should have grown up in connection with the feast of the warrior Angel is not known. Perhaps it is because people often ate and drank too much on the eve of his feast and had to blame something. The saint's feast, at the end of the harvest season, was a natural time for overindulgence; much of the hard work was done, and there was a new supply of wine (Harper, p. 243).

St. Michael's Marbles

- 2 c. oatmeal
- 1/4 c. honey
- 6 oz. raisins
- 1/2 c. peanut butter

Mix ingredients thoroughly. Roll into balls. Roll in powdered sugar and refrigerate.

— adapted from Verna Burke

October 4
St. Francis of Assisi

Francis of Assisi is one of the most cherished of all saints. The world knows the founder of the Friars Minor as a poet and through his life as a symbol of holiness. He took joy in virtue, loved all living things, and embraced poverty. All creatures were brothers and sisters to this thirteenth-century saint.

On the saint's feast, the honey almond cookies called *mostacciuoli* are on sale in all the pastry shops of Assisi in commemoration of the request for them made by the dying saint.

The saint's great love for all animals is legendary. At his request, the animals received an extra ration of feed on Christmas Eve. The custom of treating animals at Christmas stems from this. Pope John Paul II has named him patron of ecology.

In many parishes in the United States today, animals are brought to the church to be blessed on the feast of this saint.

Doggy Delights

- 1 c. flour
- 1/2 c. yeast and garlic powder
- 1/2 c. oil
- 6-8 tbsp. water
- 1/2 jar (1 1/4 oz.) sliced dried beef, chopped fine

Make a stiff dough of the first four ingredients. Add the chopped dried beef. Roll between two pieces of waxed paper till thin, about one-eighth inch. Cut into 1 1/2" squares with a sharp knife. Bake on an ungreased cookie sheet at 400 degrees for 15 to 20 minutes until cookies are hard. Cool and store in a closed container. Taste test these yourself! Cats usually like them, too.

*Yeast and garlic powder may be purchased at a health food store. This is an excellent source of vitamins and helps to repel fleas.

Yield: about 2 dozen.

October 28
Sts. Simon and Jude

According to tradition, Sts. Simon and Jude joined together in preaching the Gospel in Syria and Mesopotamia, and both were martyred in Persia. Not much is known about either saint, but St. Jude has become particularly popular in our times as the patron of hopeless cases.

In Tuscany, the people honor St. Simon by eating chestnut dishes on October 28. In England, the traditional food for this feast is dirge cakes or, as we know them, doughnuts. The circular form of the cake symbolizes eternity, without beginning or end.

Doublequick Dirge Cakes

Seven spices were baked in German honey cakes to celebrate the seven days it took for God to create the world.

- 1 can refrigerated biscuits
- 2 tsp. cinnamon
- 1/2 c. sugar
- oil for frying

Open biscuits, and with a rolling pin slightly flatten and stretch the biscuits. With your finger, make a hole in middle to form a doughnut shape. Fry in hot oil until golden brown, turning once.

In large bowl, mix cinnamon and sugar. Remove cooked dirge cake from oil with tongs and allow excess oil to drip back into pan. Put hot dirge cake in sugar mixture and turn to coat.

October 31
All Hallows' Eve
November 1
All Saints' Day
November 2
All Souls' Day
The Day of the Dead

In the old calendar, October 31 was the last day of the old year. That night was the time when all the witches and evil spirits were thought to be abroad. With the advent of Christianity, the evening was taken over as the Eve of All Hallows.

Traditional foods for Halloween include the doughnut, or dirge (soul) cake, whose round shape symbolizes eternity, without beginning or end. Apples, too, are a popular food on this day both in drink, such as cider, and in food and games. In some European countries, the custom still survives of giving away dishes made of apples. This probably stems from the old Roman feast of Pomona, the goddess of orchards and fruits. The wild outfits we wear on Halloween are a throwback to the costumes of old which were meant to keep demons at bay. The food offerings now given to trick-or-treaters are relics of food offerings once given to the dead.

All Saints Day, observed on November 1, was introduced in the seventh century to commemorate the saints and martyrs of the church, especially those who have no feast day officially designated individually in the official calendar. On this day, when prayers are said for all the saints, especially family ones, chestnut dishes are the traditional food in Italy. These dishes are of many sorts, from stuffings for roasts to cakes and candies.

All Souls Day is officially called the Commemoration of All the Faithful Departed. Popularly, this day is known in many countries as the Day of the Dead and is a time for visiting and decorating graves.

In Perugia, Italy, the town celebrates a festival that has its origins in the Middle Ages — the Fair of the Dead. Vendors come from all over Italy to set up booths and sell everything from rolling pins and pasta machines to winter underwear. Food stands are everywhere, selling hot sugared *bombe* and the confections known as *fave dei morti* (beans of the dead) or *ossi dei morti* (bones of the dead.) Vividly decorated sugar confections in the shape of skulls are also sold. In Venice, it is a day on which couples announce their engagement, and an old custom that is still observed has the suitor send his fiancée a box of *fave* cookies containing a case with the engagement ring (Barolini, p. 335).

In pre-Christian times, food was put on the graves in November, when the spirits of the dead were believed to roam the earth. Out of this came the Christian custom of baking special breads known as All Souls' bread, and making other "soul food." At the family meal in many places on this day, an extra place is set in remembrance of the departed. The food is later given to the poor. An ancient belief held that the dead came back to earth on this day, so many Central Europeans kept their windows open so that the souls in Purgatory could hear the prayers said on their behalf.

On November 1 and 2, altars are assembled throughout Mexico in honor of the departed. They are laden with flowers and sugar-candy skulls, skeleton toys, candles, photographs, bread, chocolate, and the favorite food and drink of the returning spirits. The Day of the Dead (*El Dia de los Muertos*) is a family feast that commemorates the dead and at the same time celebrates life. In Europe, the faithful prayed for the souls of the faithful departed and those in Purgatory on All Souls Day. In Spanish-Indian Mexico, this day became the day of the Dead, and the Mexicans celebrated with those who had gone before, feasted with them, and welcomed them home for a visit. On the morning of October 31, the souls of *"los angelitos,"* the little innocent ones, return. Their parents have made altars in their homes for them, and there the little ones will find their favorite sweets, toys, flowers, and candles. By noon on November 1, the children have left, and the souls of the departed adults begin to return, to feast at altars with their favorite foods.

Families go to the cemeteries and wash the tombstones. They decorate them with flowers, portraits, and refreshing drinks. Families from Oaxaca scatter marigold petals from the houses to the cemetery to aid the returning souls in finding their way home. Sand and flower petal paintings are also made in public parks, in cemeteries, and on sidewalks.

A special sweet bread made in the Valle de Bravo region is made in the form of a man, woman, or child. *Pan de Yema*, or egg bread, is another favorite for the *Muertos* altar. *Tamales*, both those cooked in corn husks and those in banana leaves, are another favorite offering for the altar. The tamales are made for the entire family, both the living and the dead.

Chicken *mole* is often served for the feast. *Mole*, which means sauce, is made in all regions of Mexico in a tempting variety. Black *mole*, which includes a number of spices and chocolate, is one of the most famous.

Tinga, a delicious and versatile meat filling, is believed to have been invented in the Santa Rosa Convent in Puebla. The nuns were the first to experiment with blending European flavors with Mexican ingredients (Quintana, p. 240). *Tinga* is wonderful served over rice, in tacos, or simply with shredded lettuce and salsa.

Chicken *Mole*

- 6 ancho chilis
- 1 chicken, cut into pieces
- 2 tbsp. vegetable oil
- 1 medium onion, chopped finely
- 2 cloves garlic, minced or mashed
- 2 tbsp. sesame seed
- 1 slice dark toast
- 1 16 oz. can whole tomatoes
- 1/2 c. raisins
- 1/4 tsp. ground cloves
- 1/2 tsp. ground cinnamon
- 1/2 tsp. ground coriander
- 1/4 tsp. ground anise
- 1 oz. unsweetened chocolate
- freshly ground black pepper
- 2 chicken bouillon cubes

Prepare the chilies. Place chilies in saucepan with just enough water to cover. Bring to a boil. Lower heat, cover, and simmer for 10 minutes. Cool. Slit open chilies, remove and discard seeds. Holding chili firmly in one hand, use a spoon to scrape the pulp from the skin. (If you cannot find these dried chilies in your area, you can substitute three level tbsp. red chili powder.)

Place prepared chilies, onion, garlic, raisins, spices, and two tbsp. sesame seed in a blender. Drain and squeeze juice out of the tomatoes, reserving juice. Add the tomatoes to chili mixture. Crumble the toast into small pieces and add to mixture. Blend to make a coarse puree.

In a medium skillet, heat the oil and pour in puree. Cook, stirring constantly, for about five minutes. Add the reserved juice from the tomatoes with enough water to make two cups, crumbled bouillon cubes, and chocolate. Continue cooking over low heat until the chocolate melts. The sauce should be a little thicker than heavy cream.

In a large glass bake dish, bake chicken at 350 degrees for 35 minutes. Reduce heat to 250 degrees. Pour *mole* sauce over chicken, cover dish with foil and continue to bake for another 30 minutes. Just before serving, sprinkle with the remaining sesame seeds. Serve over white rice.

Yield: serves 4 to 6.

(*There are many varieties of mole, and good commercial preparations of the sauce are available at import stores and grocery stores that carry a good selection of Mexican food items. Most mole recipes have a long and complex list of ingredients. If you want to attempt to make your own sauce, this recipe has been adapted for simplicity.*)

Ossi dei Morti (Dead Bone Cookies)

- 2/3 c. sugar
- 8 tbsp. margarine or butter
- 2 eggs
- 2 c. flour
- 1 1/2 tsp. vanilla extract
- 1 c. almonds, chopped fine
- confectioner's sugar

Cream the sugar, butter and eggs together. Add the flour gradually, beating until smooth. Add the vanilla and nuts, blending well. Form each teaspoon of dough into a bone or crescent shape, placing the cookies an inch apart on greased baking sheets. Bake 10 minutes in a 400-degree oven, or until the cookies are lightly browned. Dust with confectioners' sugar if desired.

Yield: 4 dozen.

Pan de Muertos (Bread of the Dead)

- 2 c. Bisquick mix
- 2 tbsp. sugar
- 1 egg
- 2/3 c. water or milk
- 10 drops anise or other flavor extract

Preheat oven to 400 degrees and grease a large cookie sheet. Mix all ingredients, beating vigorously with a spoon for 1/2 minute. Place one inch apart. Bake 20-25 minutes.

Icing:

- 2 tbsp. margarine, melted
- 1 tsp. vanilla extract
- 1 tbsp. milk
- confectioners sugar

Stir the margarine, vanilla, and milk together. Add confectioners sugar to make a thin glaze. Brush each bread with the glaze. While glaze is still wet, sprinkle with colored sugar.

Colored Sugar:

Place half c. granulated sugar in a jar with tight-fitting lid. Add two or three drops of cake coloring. Close lid and shake until the color is distributed throughout the sugar. Spread on a plate or paper to dry. Put in a salt shaker or other shaker with small holes to sprinkle. Pink is the most traditional color for this bread.

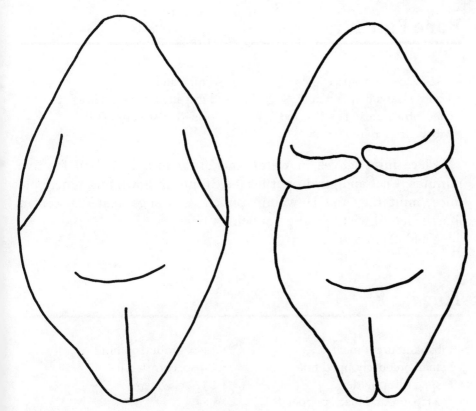

Diagram for making Mexican "Bread of the Dead." Left: make cuts on sides and foot of dough. Right: Fold "arms," define "legs," bake, and glaze with icing and pink sugar.

Bone Punch

- 1 32-oz. can pineapple juice
- 1 bottle Hawaiian punch concentrate, mixed as directed
- 2 tbsp. dried mint leaves
- 1 qt. water
- 1 can sugar cane or slices of peeled fresh cane

Place mint leaves in water and bring to a boil. Boil for five minutes. Cool and strain out leaves. In punch bowl, mix pineapple juice, mint tea, and Hawaiian punch. Cut sugar cane pieces in fourths lengthwise. Float on punch.

Yield: 2 gallons.

Tinga

- 1 lb. hamburger meat
- 1 small onion, chopped fine
- 1 tsp. garlic powder
- 1/2 tsp. ground black pepper
- 1 tsp. ground cumin
- 1 tbsp. cornstarch
- 1 1/2 c. water

Brown meat in a medium skillet. Drain off excess grease. Add chopped onion and cook over medium heat until onion is clear. Dissolve cornstarch in water and pour over meat, stirring to thicken. Add spices. Serve hot over rice or in taco shells.

Yield: 1 pound.

November 11
St. Martin of Tours
(Martinmas)

St. Martin was born during the reign of Constantine in the part of the Roman Empire which is now Hungary. He joined the imperial cavalry and was stationed in France, where he was converted to Christianity. A saintly man of God, St. Martin wanted to follow a contemplative life but was called by the citizens of Tours to be their bishop. He is most often pictured on horseback in art, shown cutting his cloak in half to share with a beggar. In his legends, that night Christ appeared to Martin dressed in that very cloak and told him that what he had done for the beggar had been done as well for Himself. This portrayal of the saint on horseback gives rise to his Spanish name, San Martín Caballero, a title much loved by his Spanish devotees.

Because his feast is celebrated on the antique feast day of the Roman god Bacchus, the god of wine and revels, St. Martin came to be known as the patron saint of drunkards, and even today we hear that someone thoroughly intoxicated is "Martin drunk." It is still customary in winemaking regions of Italy to taste new wine on St. Martin's Day.

This day was the last religious feast day before the beginning of Advent, which in earlier times was a period of fasting. Thus, the day is generally observed throughout Europe as a day of thanksgiving and a day to celebrate the harvest. The traditional main dish is a goose. This is, by legend, because when the citizens of Tours were seeking the saint to become their bishop, he tried to hide, but his hiding place was revealed by a goose.

Plato de San Martín Caballero

- 1 lb. ground meat
- 1 c. yellow cornmeal
- 1/2 c. bacon drippings
- 2 eggs, well beaten
- 1 can cream-style yellow corn
- 1 c. milk
- 1 onion
- 1/2 lb. cheddar cheese, grated
- 3 jalapeño peppers, chopped fine
- 1 small jar pimiento peppers
- 3/4 tsp. salt
- 1/2 tsp. soda

Sauté meat until browned and crumbly. Drain off excess grease. Mix corn meal, milk, eggs, creamed corn, bacon drippings, salt, and soda.

Grease large iron skillet. Heat. Sprinkle two tbsp. cornmeal butter in skillet and let it brown slightly, stirring constantly. Pour half the batter in the skillet. Sprinkle cheese evenly over batter. Sprinkle meat over cheese. Next sprinkle the onion and finally the peppers. Pour remaining batter on top. Bake at 350 degrees for 45 to 50 minutes.

Yield: serves 4 to 6.

Thanksgiving

Thanksgiving is not a Catholic feast, but to American Catholics it has religious overtones. To Catholics, Thanksgiving means the appreciation due to God for all the good things of life, especially family and food. The Thanksgiving in Plymouth Colony in 1621 was not the first service of Thanksgiving in North America. Ponce de León gave thanks in Florida in 1513. In 1578, English settlers in Newfoundland proclaimed a day of thanksgiving, and in 1607 another was observed by the Popham Colony on what is now the coast of Maine. Today's Thanksgiving was established as a national holiday by congressional action in 1941.

It was the Pilgrims' Thanksgiving in Massachusetts, however, that set the pattern for our present celebration. It was here, too, that the unfortunate turkey became the traditional Thanksgiving bird. Governor Bradford had sent out four men to bring in some game for the community feast. They happened to find wild turkeys, but could as easily have brought venison, boar, or rabbit. Friendly Indians nearby brought venison, and what started out as one solemn day of thanksgiving lengthened into three days of games and feasting. They did stop occasionally for Psalm singing (Harper p. 301).

Luis de Torres, a Jewish physician who sailed with Columbus, is credited with giving the turkey its name. When he saw the strange big fowl for the first time, he said, *"tukki,"* which is the Hebrew word for "big bird." His exclamation was mistaken for a name by his non-Jewish companions, and the name has stuck ever since.

December 4
St. Barbara

The Syrian Christmas begins on St. Barbara's Day and continues until Epiphany, January 6. A table of sweetmeats prepared from nuts, sugar, honey, and wheat is prepared in memory of the dead and signifies the resurrection. On the eve of the feast, the little Syrian children are taught lessons of unselfishness and thoughtfulness for others less fortunate. When the neighbors and friends and relatives meet to celebrate, all kinds of pastry such as *Buklawa, Burma*, and *Bkhout* as well as many kinds of candy are prepared. Enough of the traditional wheat porridge is cooked to serve all the guests, and the host tells the story of St. Barbara to his guests. After the wheat is cooked, the hostess removes it from the fire and mixes sugar, rose water, and candy into it.

In Southern France, grain is the symbol of the day and is used as a table decoration as well as food.

Nut Tarts

Crust
- 1 3-oz. pkg. cream cheese
- 1 c. flour
- 1/2 c. butter or margarine

Filling
- 1 egg
- 3/4 c. brown sugar
- 1 tbsp. melted butter
  1 tsp. vanilla
- pinch of salt
- 2/3 c. chopped nuts

Mix well. Divide into 12 cups of an ungreased muffin tin. Flour your fingers if necessary and press around to make shells.

Beat egg and sugar together. Mix in melted butter, vanilla, and salt. Divide nuts evenly into shells. Pour filling over nuts. Bake at 325 for 30 minutes. Cook tarts before removing from tins. Top each with whipped cream before serving.

Yield: 12 tarts.

— Verna Burke

December 6
St. Nicholas Day

December 6 is a great day for happiness and celebration for the children of Germany and Belgium. They have a Christmas tree, and St. Nicholas makes a preliminary visit to their homes the night before. He is dressed as a bishop and accompanied by his mischievous helper Krampus. Good children are given apples or candy, and naughty ones are switched. Figures of Krampus made of wired prunes and of Nicolo made of figs and marshmallows are favorite decorations in homes and shop windows. As soon as St. Nicholas leaves, the children put their shoes or baskets around the room. They leave out water, hay, carrots, and a potato for St. Nicholas's horse. The next day, the room is in disorder, showing that the saint has been there, and the good children find sweetmeats and playthings.

Holland and Belgium have special forms of cakes and sweetmeats for the St. Nicholas season. In Holland these are flat, hard cakes called *Klaasjes*, once made exclusively in the form of a bishop and his horse to honor Bishop St. Nicholas but now made in all shapes. In certain places, the figure of the saint is baked in dough with currant eyes. *Letterbanket* is made in the form of letters so that one may order his name in cake. *Oliebollen*, the national pastries of Holland, are served on St. Nicholas' Eve. Apple fritters, often made with beer and sprinkled generously with vanilla sugar, are also served.

The Hollanders brought the custom of the visit of St. Nicholas to America. Later, when New Amsterdam became New York, this Dutch tradition of "Sinter Claas" was transferred to Christmas and the figure of the saint changed into the present legendary figure of Santa Claus.

Bischofsbrot

- 6 eggs — separated
- 2/3 c. sugar
- 1 c. flour
- 2/3 c. almonds, blanched and slivered
- 1 c. raisins
- 1/2 c. chopped candied citrus peel
- 6 oz. sweet cooking chocolate cut into small pieces (or substitute toll house morsels)

Beat egg yolks until light and creamy. Beat in the sugar. Stir in flour and almonds, raisins, citrus peel, and chocolate. Fold in egg whites which have been beaten stiff. Pour into a greased, floured loaf pan and bake in a slow oven, 300 degrees, for an hour. Let the bread stand 24 hours and serve in very thin slices.

Yield: 1 loaf.

Bishop's Wine

- 1 bottle burgundy wine
- 1 stick cinnamon, broken
- 3/4 c. sugar
- 2 tbsp. grated orange rind

Heat all ingredients to the boiling point. Serve hot. Garnish with a cinnamon stick or with a slice of orange.

Yield: 1 bottle.

December 13
St. Lucy

In Sweden St. Lucy's Day is celebrated on December 13. The prettiest or oldest girl in the house impersonates Lucy. She dresses in white with a red sash and wears a wire crown on her head covered with bilberry twigs. In her crown there are nine lighted candles. She goes through the house very early on Christmas morning, awakening all sleepers and giving each a cup of coffee or a sweet drink and offering a platter of beautiful pastries.

Saffransbrod, or saffron buns, are the favorite offerings. The buns are made in many shapes, each with its own designation. The Lucia Cats, or *Lussekatter*, are the most popular. Some of these are set aside and crumbled into the seeds for the next season's grain planting to symbolize the life cycle.

Other popular shapes for the *saffransbrod* are the *julgalt* (Christmas), *praestens har* (Priests' Hair) and *Luciakrona* (Lucy crown) as well as the standard *julbrod*, or braid.

Although Sweden is most famous for the celebration and customs of Santa Lucia, the saint and the festivity are of old Sicilian origin. Saint Lucy embodies a theme of light, sight, and renewed hope. The little virgin martyr is patroness for the blind and is often shown in art with her eyes on a plate. This is from her legend, in which she was blinded by her torturers.

Although saffron is the preferred spice for breads baked in honor of St. Lucy in Sweden, the Italians prefer the flavor of cardamum, including it in muffins, wine and sometimes even coffee on this feast. Today's bakers may prefer the Italian spice preference due to the fact that saffron is the most expensive spice on the market.

A legend tells that during a great famine the Syracusans invoked the aid of Santa Lucia. While they were praying, a ship carrying grain came into the harbor and saved the city. Thus a wheat dish is traditionally eaten on December 13 to recall the miracle.

In Syracuse, Sicily, another festa for Santa Lucia takes place on May 1. Again her coffin is moved in procession under a shower of flowers. Again, a wheat dish is served to recall the miracle.

Light-of-Lucy Rice

- 1 tsp. Mexican saffron
- 1/2 c. water
- 3 tbsp. oil
- 1 c. rice
- 2/3 c. frozen mixed vegetables
- 1/2 tsp. ground white pepper
- salt to taste

The slang use of the word "lettuce" to mean "money" may go way back to a story told about Pope Sixtus V, who once sent a salad to an impoverished lawyer, a friend of his. The man had determined to go and ask the Pope for aid but fell ill on the way. The Pope sent word that he would send a salad that would cure him. Sixtus dispatched a messenger with a basket of lettuce. When the lawyer opened the heads, he found them filled with money.

Place one tsp. Mexican saffron in half c. water and heat to boil. Remove from heat to cool. Pour through paper towel into a two-c. measure, straining out stamens. Add water to make two cups.

In a medium skillet, put oil and rice. Cook over medium high heat, stirring constantly, until rice begins to turn a golden brown. Quickly add saffron water, vegetables and seasoning. Bring to a boil. Reduce heat to low, cover, and simmer for 15 minutes.

Yield: serves 4.

December 17
Virgen de la Soledad
(Virgin of Solitude)

In Mexico, a plump little fritter or doughnut called a *buñuelo* is served all through the Christmas season. These are a big feature of the celebration of the Virgin of Solitude, Oaxaca's patron saint. Customers buy the plate in which these are served and smash it on the ground after they have eaten the cake.

Buñuelos

- 1/4 c. margarine
- 4 c. flour
- 1/4 tsp. salt
- 1 1/2 tbsp. sugar
- 1 egg, beaten

- 3 tsp. anise seed
- 4 tsp. ground cinnamon
- 4 tbsp. sugar
- 1 c. water

Boil anise seed in water. Set aside to steep. Strain out seeds. Blend the dry ingredients with the shortening. Add beaten egg and lukewarm "tea" to dry ingredients and knead the dough. Make small balls of the dough. Cover and let stand for 15 to 30 minutes. Roll the dough out as thin as possible. Fry in deep fat or oil until golden brown and crisp. Toss the fried *buñuelos* in a paper sack with the ground cinnamon and sugar to coat the cookies with the sugar-spice mixture.

December 26
St. Stephen's Day

December 26 is St. Stephen's day. In England, it is known as Boxing Day, and its origin antedates Christmas and is traced to a Roman custom of giving and receiving presents during the Saturnalia. In England, on this day, gifts are given, usually in money, to tradesmen. A box was taken aboard every vessel that sailed out of port near Christmas, and contributions were dropped into it. The box was opened when the ship reached home port. The money was generally used as a contribution to some needy person, who had a Mass said for the mariners (Hottes, p. 233). A special cake known as Boxing Day Cake is traditionally served on this day.

In Finland, gifts of food, wine, and clothing are exchanged on this day.

St. Stephen was the first Christian martyr. He is the patron saint of horses, and they figure prominently in his feast. In Italy, roasted chestnuts are eaten on the saint's day. Bread shaped like horseshoes is baked on that day.

Stephen's patronage of horses may be based on the fact that in pre-Christian times horses were sacrificed at the winter solstice among the Germanic nations. A poem from the tenth century pictures the saint as owner of a horse which is miraculously cured by our Lord. In many rural sections of Europe, it was and sometimes still is customary to bless horses in front of the church on this day. Formerly, water, salt, oats, and hay were also blessed to be kept by the farmers and fed to their horses in case of sickness (Kaufman, p. 73).

Domaci' Vino (Homemade Wine)

- 8 c. grapes
- 4 c. sugar
- 1 gal. boiling water

Take a clean one-gallon glass jar with a good lid. Use wild grapes or grapes you have in your area. Wash well. Fill jar with grapes and sugar. Add boiling water to within one inch of the top. tighten lid and leave in a dark place to ferment till grape seeds, skins, etc. drop to the bottom, at which time the wine is ready for use. Decant carefully, pouring through a cloth, so as not to disturb the sludge on bottom.

December 27
St. John the Evangelist

The feast of St. John the Evangelist, the apostle known also as the beloved disciple or St. John the Divine, is celebrated on December 27. Wine is a part of the remembrance of the feast, and on that day there is a special blessing of wine in recognition of the legend of the saint's having survived a poisoned wine that had been served to him. The wine is symbolic of the great love of Christ that filled the saint's heart; he alone of the apostles remained with Our Lord during the Crucifixion, according to popular tradition.

In Catholic sections of Europe, St. John's wine is blessed by the local priest or is sprinkled with holy water by the head of the family. It is served with the main meal on the saint's feast, and even the youngest children receive a small portion of it.

St. John's Wine

- 1 qt. red wine
- 1 c. water
- 1/2 c. sugar
- 3 whole cloves
- 2 cinnamon sticks, broken into pieces
- 3 cardamom seed
- 1/2 tsp. whole allspice

Tie spices in a small piece of cloth. Boil spices and sugar in water for a few minutes or until water is half the original volume. Pour spice mix and wine into a large pan and heat to boiling. Serve hot.

Yield: 1 quart.

December 28
Feast of the Holy Innocents

From the eleventh century, the feast of the Holy Innocents — the children who were slain for Christ by Herod — was celebrated as a special day for children. It became a custom, not only in the homes of the faithful but also in convents and monasteries, to serve some form of "baby food" to the youngest ones at the evening meal. This included children in families and novices in religious houses. Generally this was some sort of pabulum to which were often added spices or fruit (Kauffman, p. 77).

Stewed Prunes

- 12 oz. pkg. dried, pitted prunes
- grated rind of 1 lemon
- 2 c. water
- 1 stick cinnamon, broken in pieces
- 1 tbsp. sugar

In a medium saucepan, put sugar, cinnamon, and lemon rind. Add two cups of water. Bring to rapid boil and boil for two minutes. Remove cinnamon pieces. Add prunes. Add enough more water just to cover fruit. Return to boil. Boil one minute. Cover and remove from heat. Let set for five minutes before serving.

Yield: serves 6.

Special Occasions

Baptism/ Christening

The first feast experienced by a new soul in the world is often the joyous feast of baptism or christening.

The expression "born with a silver spoon in his mouth" originated in connection with this sacrament. In the Middle Ages, it was the custom for godparents at baptisms to give spoons to their new godchildren. Naturally, the richer the godparent the more precious the metal of the spoon. Children of wealthy parents already had all the silver they needed; thus, they were "born with a silver spoon in their mouths" and did not need the gift of their godparent. The usual baptismal spoon was an "apostle" spoon — one made with an apostle carved on the handle. Lavish godparents gave the child the complete set of twelve.

In Mexico, after the christening at the parish church, in which the child's stain of original sin is removed and he is named and welcomed to the community, the godfather distributes the *bolas* and tosses into the air coins of various denominations to symbolize the fruits of fortune that he hopes will attend the child throughout his or her life.

Then the infant's parents gather with the godparents, the priest, and family friends to break bread together and celebrate by eating the *antojitos* (little whims or hors d'oeuvres of Mexico) or perhaps a feast with many courses. Sweets shine with a special brilliance.

Cheese Straws

- 1 c. flour
- 1 c. grated Parmesan cheese
- 1 c. margarine
- salt and pepper

Prepare the pastry with the ingredients. Roll out and cut into strips approximately two inches by one half inch. Put on a baking sheet and bake at 400 degrees for 10 minutes or until golden.

Yield: about 1 dozen.

— Dr. Abe Goldfarb

Tasty Trash

- 12 oz. box Golden Grahams or Rice Chex
- 12 oz. pkg. raisins
- 3 c. roasted and shelled peanuts
- 2 c. peanut butter
- 12 oz. pkg. chocolate bits
- 1 lb. powdered sugar

Mix cereal, raisins, and nuts in large bowl. Over low heat, melt peanut butter and chocolate bits together. Pour over cereal mixture, stirring to coat pieces well. Empty sugar into large paper bag. Pour in mixture and shake well until all mixture is coated and sugar is used up. Store in sealed container.

— Diana Littlefield

Hot Shrimp Toast

- 1 lb. raw shrimp, peeled
- 15 oz. can water chestnuts, drained
- 1/4 c. chopped green onion tops
- 2 tsp. salt
- 1 tsp. sugar
- 1 beaten egg

Put all ingredients in a blender and grind to make a paste. Spread on 15 slices of thin-sliced white bread. Sprinkle lightly with fine bread crumbs.

Cut each slice into 4 triangles. Heat oil in a frying pan so the oil is one inch deep and very hot. Fry each triangle, shrimp side down first. Then brown on other side. Drain on towels.

Yield: makes 60.

— Verna Burke

Onion Stock

- 5 tbsp. butter or margarine
- 1/2 large onion, sliced very thin
- 1/4 tsp. black Pepper
- 1 tbsp. flour
- 2 beef bouillon cubes
- 3 c. water
- 1 tbsp. Worcestershire sauce
- 10 drops tabasco sauce

Sauté onions in butter until they begin to brown. Sprinkle flour over mix, and stir to dissolve flour and make a thin roux. Add other ingredients and bring to a boil. Reduce heat and cook for ten minutes. Use as stock when preparing meat dishes or serve as a mildly spicy soup for two.

Yield: 2 1/2 cups.

Bea's Best *Quiche*

- 6 oz. swiss cheese, grated
- 8 slices bacon, cooked and crumbled
- 3 eggs
- 1 c. whipping cream
- 1/2 c. milk

- 1/2 tsp. salt
- 1/4 tsp. black pepper
- dash cayenne pepper
- 1/2 tsp. mustard powder
- 9" unbaked pie shell

Sprinkle cheese and bacon in crust. Beat all other ingredients until smooth. Pour into pie shell. Bake at 375 degrees for 45 minutes. Serve with spinach or green salad.

Yield: serves 4 to 6.

— Bea Whitfil

Broccoli-Rice Casserole

- 1 c. minute rice
- 2 pkgs. frozen chopped broccoli
- 1 can cream of chicken soup, undiluted
- 1 can cream of mushroom soup, undiluted

- 8 oz. Cheese Whiz
- 1 c. chopped celery
- 3/4 c. chopped onion
- 1 stick margarine

Saute margarine, celery, and onion. Add broccoli, rice, soups, and cheese. Mix until cheese melts. Pour into 13 x 9-inch casserole. Bake at 350 degrees for one hour.

Yield: serves 8 to 12.

— Betsy Altenburger

Pan de Polvo

- 2 lbs. flour
- 1 lb. shortening
- 1/3 c. cinnamon & anise tea
- 1/4 tsp. yeast
- 7 oz. sugar
- pinch of salt
- cinnamon and sugar to coat

Mix flour and salt together and set aside. Mix the shortening and the sugar. Add yeast to the tea and mix it into the shortening-sugar mix. Blend until the mix is smooth and creamy. Add the flour to make a soft dough. Separate the dough into small, soft dough balls, ready to individually roll out and cut into cookies with small-size cookie cutter. Bake on ungreased cookie sheet at 350 degrees for 10 to 12 minutes or until lightly brown. Roll warm cookies in a mix of cinnamon and sugar.

— Consuela Martínez

Lace Cookies

- 1/2 c. powdered sugar
- 1/2 c. flour
- 1/4 c. blanched almonds, finely chopped
- 2 egg whites
- 2 tsp. vanilla

Cream butter and sugar, add egg whites and flour. Mix well and add vanilla and almonds. Drop in rounds on a cookie sheet and bake at 350 degrees for 15 to 20 minutes until golden. At the door of the oven, roll them quickly round a pencil to form little tubes. Place on a plate and dust with powdered sugar.

— Dr. Abe Goldfarb

Picadillo Cubano (Cuban Hash)

- 3/4 lb. sausage
- 2 lbs. ground beef
- 3/4 lb. ground pork
- 3 tsp. salt
- 3/4 tsp. ground black pepper
- 3/4 c. dry sherry
- 3/4 c. olive oil
- 4 cloves garlic, minced
- 2 large onions, chopped
- 2 medium green peppers, chopped
- 1/2 bottle capers
- 1 c. pitted black olives
- 2 large bay leaves
- dash of cumin
- dash oregano
- 1 6-oz. can tomato paste
- 1 c. raisins
- 1 c. blanched almonds, chopped or slivered

Mix beef and pork with salt and pepper. Add sherry and let stand 2 hours. Brown sausage, drain and set aside. Saute garlic, onions, pepper, capers and olives in oil in heavy skillet until lightly browned. Add meat, tomato paste, raisins, spices, almonds and sausage. Cook for 1 hour over low heat.

Yield: serves 6 to 10.

— JoAnn Hawkins

Name-Day Celebrations

A name day commemorates the feast of the saint whose name we received at baptism, or the saint we have chosen as patron.

The day of the saint's death, and thus his birth into Heaven, is the day generally celebrated as his feast. In some countries and in most religious orders, name days are celebrated rather than birthdays. Name days can be a means of strengthening the faith of our children and of drawing them closer in the Communion of Saints (McLaughlin, pp. 11-13). In annually commemorating our patrons, we can draw closer to them as our inspiration and as our friend.

Celebrating the name days of the family members' patrons can become a beautiful tradition for your own family. There are no hard and fast rules for these celebrations, and they can be personalized for each family.

The celebration could begin on the vigil of the feast day with a family rosary or other prayer. On the day of the feast itself, the family might attend Mass together and later have a sort of party with friends. Special decorations, using symbols of the saint, and an elaborate dessert might be served. Games in honor of the saint could be played. A small home altar to the saint might be set up; a special prayer asking the patron's protection and help for the name-day celebrant should be said. Children love ceremony and tradition, and your own family decorations and ideas should be carefully preserved from year to year. Consult your Church calendar for the days to celebrate for your family's own special patrons. A good beginning is to go to your church or school library with your child and find as much as you can about his or her patron. A classic Catholic book from the early 1960s by Helen McLaughlin, called *My Nameday, Come for Dessert,* has hundreds of ideas for nameday celebrations.

Food customs connected with the celebration of the feasts of some of the saints are given in this book. If your saint is not listed, then begin your own traditions in his or her honor.

In Germany, there is a traditional German name-day cake called *Kugelhupf.*

Kugelhupf

- 1/2 c. milk
- water
- 1 pkg. yeast
- 1/2 c. sugar
- 1 tsp. salt
- flour
- 2 eggs
- 1/2 c. melted margarine
- 1/2 c. chopped raisins
- 1 tsp. lemon rind
- margarine to grease pan
- 15 or 16 blanched almonds
- 2 tbsp. bread crumbs or finely ground almonds

In a mixing bowl, pour a half cup of scalded milk, cool until warm. As the milk cools, soften yeast in a quarter cup of warm water. Add sugar, salt, and 1 1/2 cups of flour, mixing well. Add dissolved yeast and beat until smooth. Add eggs, beating thoroughly. Add melted margarine and beat with electric mixer on medium speed about five minutes. Scrape batter down from the sides of the bowl, cover and let rise to double, about an hour and a half.

While the batter rises, prepare the pan. Use a two-pint cake mold or a seven-inch angel-cake pan. Grease pan generously with margarine and sprinkle two tbsp. of fine bread crumbs or finely ground almonds in pan, shaking to coat the inside of the pan with crumbs. Arrange almonds in a design in the bottom of the pan.

When batter has doubled, stir it down and mix in chopped raisins and grated lemon rind. Spoon batter carefully on top of almonds. Cover and let rise again to double, about an hour and a quarter. Bake in a moderate oven, 350 degrees, for 45 to 50 minutes. Check after 15 minutes, and if cake is turning brown, lay a piece of foil over cake for rest of baking time. When done, turn out onto a wire cake rack to cool. Dust with powdered sugar if you wish. A design can be made on the top of the cake by putting a scalloped paper doily on the cake and sifting powdered sugar on the cake. Then remove the doily.

Seven-Minute Frosting

- 2 egg whites
- 1 1/2 cups sugar
- 5 tbsp. cold water

- 1/4 tsp. cream of tartar
- 1 1/2 tsp. light corn syrup
- 1 1/4 tsp. vanilla

In the top of a double boiler, beat all ingredients except vanilla until thoroughly blended. Place over rapidly boiling water. Beat constantly with a rotary beater or a wire whisk for seven minutes. Remove icing from heat and add vanilla. Continue beating until the frosting is of the right consistency to spread.

Yield: frosts 1 two-layer cake.

First Communion/ Confirmation

First Communion and Confirmation are milestone events in the life of a Catholic. In addition to the Mass, a celebration with family, friends, godparents, and sponsors is called for. The celebration can be a simple breakfast or brunch, or an elaborate dinner, depending on the time of the Mass, the means of the family, and the number of persons to be included. Some families choose to celebrate these occasions by having a meal in a restaurant; others spend days preparing homemade specialties.

Sesame Cheese Block

- 1/2 c. sesame seed
- 1 8-oz. pkg. cream cheese
- 1 tbsp. Worcestershire or barbecue sauce

Put sesame seed in a small skillet over medium high heat. Stir constantly until seeds are toasted and brown. Remove from heat and pour seed on a plate. Roll block of cheese in seed to cover completely. Place coated cheese and extra seed on a small serving plate. Drizzle Worcestershire sauce over top of block. Serve with crackers. Barbecue sauce can be substituted for the Worcestershire.

— Verna Burke

Refrigerator Pickles

- 1 lb. cucumbers, peeled and sliced
- 1/2 onion, sliced
- 1/2 c. sugar
- 1 tbsp. salt
- 1 tsp. celery seed
- 1 tsp. mustard seed
- white vinegar

Fill jar with cucumbers. Add other ingredients. Cover with cold vinegar. Seal and shake until sugar and salt are dissolved. Let stand 24 hours in refrigerator before serving.

Yield: 1 quart.

— Verna Burke

Cream of Pumpkin Soup

- 2 lbs. pumpkin, seeds removed
- 1 large onion, chopped
- 4 c. water
- 4 beef or chicken bouillon cubes
- 1/2 c. grated parmesan cheese

- 3 tbsp. margarine
- 1/4 tsp. garlic powder
- 1 c. evaporated milk
- 1 tsp. cornstarch

In a large saucepan bring the water to a boil. Add bouillon cubes, stirring to dissolve. Cut up the pumpkin and cook in the stock until tender. Liquify the cooked pumpkin in a blender. Sauté the onion in the margarine. Add the onion, spices, and the pureed pumpkin to the broth, stirring to blend. Dissolve cornstarch in a small amount of water and add to soup. Add the milk. Bring to a boil and cook for a few minutes to allow soup to thicken slightly. Add the cheese. Serve with croutons.

Yield: serves 6 to 8.

Molinaro Sauce

- 5 medium tomatoes, chopped
- 2 tsp. oil
- 3/4 c. onion
- 1 tsp. crushed garlic
- 1 c. chicken broth (or substitute vegetable broth)

- 1 1/4 tsp. thyme
- 1/2 tsp. salt
- 1/2 tsp. black pepper
- 1/2 c. sliced black olives
- 1 9-oz. can tomato sauce

In a heavy pan, place oil and onion. Cook over medium heat until onions are clear. Add garlic. Stir in chicken broth, thyme, salt, pepper, and tomato sauce. Cook, uncovered, until tomatoes are tender. Stir in olives. Serve over cooked pasta of your choice.

Yield: serves 6.

— Ann Molinaro

57th Dynasty Oriental Kabobs

- 4 chicken breasts, de-boned and cut in small chunks
- 12 small ripe olives, pitted
- 12 small fresh mushrooms, washed
- 1 bell pepper, cut in pieces
- 1 medium onion, cut in pieces
- 8" wooden skewers

String ingredients for kabobs on skewers to make small kabobs.

Sauce:

- 1/2 c. Heinz 57 Sauce
- 2 tbsp. margarine, melted
- 4 tbsp. soy sauce
- 2 tbsp. orange marmalade (or substitute grape jelly)
- 1 tbsp. vinegar
- 1/8 tsp. garlic powder

Mix all ingredients for sauce. Place kabobs on cookie pan. Spoon sauce over kabobs. Broil until chicken is well cooked, about 15 minutes. Baste several times during cooking, and serve the extra sauce with the kabobs.

Yield: 12 kabobs.

Zucchini Casserole

- 3 large zucchini squash, sliced
- 1 tsp. salt
- 1/2 c. uncooked rice
- 3/4 c. water
- 1 large can of tomatoes, mashed in juice
- 1/2 large onion, chopped
- 2 c. grated cheddar cheese

Generously butter a deep casserole dish. Layer the ingredients (except cheese) in dish, beginning and ending with the squash. Cover and cook in a 350-degree oven for one hour. Remove from oven and cover with cheese. Return to oven and bake uncovered for five minutes.

Yield: serves 6.

— Helen Nixon

Fudge Cake Squares

Cake:
- 1 c. butter or margarine
- 4 eggs
- 1/3 c. powdered cocoa
- 2 c. sugar
- 1 1/2 c. flour
- pinch of salt
- 1 pkg. miniature marshmallows

Icing:
- 1/2 stick butter or margarine
- 1 box powdered sugar
- 1/3 c. cocoa
- 1 tsp. vanilla
- 1/3 c. milk
- 1 c. chopped, toasted pecans (optional)
- 1 pinch salt

Melt one c. margarine. Add eggs, one-third c. cocoa, sugar, flour and salt. Stir to mix and pour into cookie pan. Bake 15 to 20 minutes at 350 degrees. Sprinkle on marshmallows. Return to oven just long enough for the marshmallows to melt. Heat the rest of the ingredients until they begin to bubble. Pour over cake while hot. Let cool and cut into squares.

(This recipe is quick, easy, and best of all, only uses two pans.)

Syrup Pie

- 3 eggs
- 1/2 c. syrup
- pinch of salt
- 1/2 c. sugar
- 1/2 c. buttermilk
- 1 tsp. vanilla

Lightly beat eggs. Add remaining ingredients, stirring to mix. Pour in unbaked pie shell. Bake at 350 degrees until center is set and knife inserted comes out clean.

Approximately 45 minutes baking time. If desired, top with meringue or a fruit topping.

Yield: 1 nine-inch pie.

— Vennie Triana

Vennie's Prize Pie Dough

- 2 c. sifted floor
- 3/4 c. Crisco, packed
- 1 tsp. salt
- 5 tbsp. ice-cold water

Mix all ingredients without working the dough too hard. Roll out on floured surface.

— Vennie Triana

The *Quinceanera*

The *Quinceanera* is a Catholic celebration familiar to those in the Southwestern United States and wherever those of Spanish descent reside. It is a traditional celebration of a young girl's fifteenth birthday.

The special Mass and service are beautiful. The girl renews the promises made for her at baptism, and the priest reminds her that she has now become a woman. She prays that God's graces will not be wasted in her, and takes Our Lady as her model, her strength, and her guide.

After the Mass, a joyous fiesta is held. Mariachi musicians play, and there is an elaborate feast, including a cake, which is generally larger and more elaborate than most American wedding cakes. Champagne or punch is served. Barbecue is one of the most common foods; this main course is sometimes catered and sometimes prepared by friends and relatives of the honoree. The happy feasting and dancing continues throughout the night.

Jalapeño Jelly Cheese Block

- 3/4 c. ground bell pepper
- 1/4 c. ground jalapeños
- 1 c. cider vinegar
- 5 c. sugar
- 6 oz. liquid pectin
- few drops green or red food color

Grind peppers in blender or food processor. Mix all ingredients except pectin and coloring in a pan. Bring to a boil and boil four minutes. Cool one minute. Add pectin and a few drops of food color. Pour into clean jars and refrigerate until use. Makes approximately two cups.

Place block of cream cheese on a small serving plate. Spoon jelly over cheese. Serve with crackers to spread.

— Bea Whitfil

Artichoke Dip

- 1 can artichoke hearts, drained and mashed
- 1/4 c. Parmesan cheese

- 1 tbsp. Worcestershire sauce
- 1/2 tsp. garlic salt
- 2 tbsp. mayonnaise

Mix all ingredients. Chill before serving. Serve with potato or corn chips.

Pickled Okra

- 1 pt. white vinegar
- 1 pt. water
- 1/2 tbsp. sugar
- 1/2 c. salt
- 1 tsp. dill seed per jar

- 1 clove garlic per jar
- 1 small hot red pepper (optional) per jar
- fresh tender okra

Place washed okra in sterilized jars with point down. Add garlic, dill seed, and pepper to each jar. Put vinegar, water, sugar, and salt in pan and bring to a boil. Pour hot vinegar over okra. Seal and let set at least a week before serving. Best when served cold.

— Glen Burleson

Six-Layer Dip

- 1st layer: 3 avocados, mashed well
- 1 tsp. garlic powder
- 1/2 tsp. lemon
- 2 tbsp. mayonnaise
- salt and pepper to taste

Mix above together well and spread on tray, making a one-inch rim around edge of mixture.

- 2nd layer: 8 oz. sour cream
- 3rd layer: small jar picante sauce
- 4th layer: 1 small can sliced black olives, drained
- 5th layer: 2 fresh tomatoes, chopped
- 6th layer: 1 lb. cheddar cheese, grated fine

Cover tray with plastic wrap and refrigerate a few hours before serving. Serve with corn chips.

— Glen Burleson

Why don't we eat meat when we fast on Friday? In the old days, people believed meat stimulated the passions. Therefore, anyone who was trying to develop his spiritual nature and to conquer his fleshly lusts would be greatly helped by going without meat.

Sopa de Tortillas Migas

- 1/4 lb. ground meat
- 12 corn tortillas
- 4 oz. green chili
- 1 c. fresh tomatoes, chopped
- 1 c. grated cheese
- 1/2 c. onions, chopped
- 1/2 c. soup stock (or 1 bouillon cube dissolved in hot water)

Cut the tortillas into three-quarter-inch strips. Saute the onions, add tomato and garlic powder with meat and green chili. Place the dry tortillas in a casserole dish. Add the soup stock and the meat mixture. Bake in a 350 degree oven for 20 minutes.

Yield: serves 2 to 4.

— Roland Contreras

(There are two types of soup in Mexican-Indian cooking. The liquid soup dish is called "caldo," and the more solid carbohydrate dish is known as "sopa." The name of this sopa literally translates to "little pieces of tortilla soup.")

Butter-Baked Fish

- 2 large fish filets
- 1/2 lime
- butter

- pepper and salt to taste
- onion flakes
- oregano

Put fish filets in heavy foil. Squeeze lime onto fish and dot with butter. Sprinkle salt, pepper, onion flakes, and oregano on filets. Seal with foil. Bake in a 350-degree oven for 20 minutes.

Yield: serves 2.

— Isabelle Medina

Rocky Road Bars

- 10 marshmallows, quartered
- 1/2 c. broken walnuts or pecans

- 1/2 lb. German sweet chocolate

Line bottom of 9 x 14-inch loaf pan with waxed paper, letting paper extend in two-inch tabs on all sides. Arrange marshmallows in pan and fill spaces between marshmallows with nuts. Heat chocolate in double boiler over boiling water until partly melted; then remove from boiling water and stir rapidly until entirely melted. Pour over contents of pan using fork to distribute chocolate throughout. Tap pan several times to settle chocolate. Let stand in cool place to harden. Run sharp knife around sides of pan and lift candy out with paper tabs. Cut in one-by-two-inch pieces.

Yield: 18 small pieces.

— Verna Burke

Weddings

Eating together is very deeply laid in the marriage rites. Men and women had been living together in a union regulated by custom and law for generations before the Church added her sacramental seal, and food was always a part of the ceremony of marriage. In ancient Rome, the bride's father gave a great feast for the guests. In Greece, after the procession to the bride's house, she was greeted with a shower of dates, figs, and other fertility fruits.

Originally, Christian wedding breakfasts were held because the contracting parties had been fasting in order to receive Communion as a completion of the bond of their union. The final meal was the marriage feast, eaten after the ceremony had concluded. This banquet has generally been associated with the nuptial procession of the bride to and from the place of the marriage rite. Also in connection with this procession is the widespread custom of throwing grain or fruit on the bridal pair. This is clearly the remnant of a fertility rite.

Each part of the Christian world has its own wedding customs, including the foods which are served at this once-in-a-lifetime event. Foods tend to be elaborate, and sweetness and richness are emphasized.

Mary Bednarz remembers vividly the wedding of a cousin in the rural south of Poland in the late 1970s. By nine A.M., over twenty horse-drawn wagons were parked outside the groom's house. Both the wagon and horse were gaily decorated, and one wagon was reserved for a band which played all the way. After a large breakfast, the guests piled aboard and the wagons went in procession to pick up the bride. After the ceremony at church, the procession went to the bride's home again, this time for a large dinner.

Outside of the church, the "raggedy men" stood, waiting for a donation; the wise wagoner passed a coin to the beggars, or else he might not be allowed through.

Three hundred people assembled at the bride's home, presenting the newlyweds with gifts of chickens, pigs, bread, and eggs. A large, rich dinner was served, along with homemade wine. A fruit compote, a non-alcoholic punch with whole fruit in it, was reserved for the children. The table groaned with potato salad, kielbasa, pickled eggs, herring, and other specialties of the area. The festivities continued until late in the evening.

JoAnn Thomas comes from an Italian heritage. She remembers a special cookie baked by her mother that was served at many celebrations, especially weddings. The cookies, called Italian Wedding Rings, were made in a round shape to symbolize eternity. They were thought to bring good luck to the persons being honored and to all those gathered for the festivities.

Mexican Wedding Cookies

- 1 c. margarine
- 8 tbsp. powdered sugar
- 2 c. flour
- 2 c. chopped pecans
- 1/2 c. tiny chocolate pieces (optional)
- 1 tsp. vanilla

Cream together margarine and powdered sugar. Add flour, nuts and vanilla, blending with hands. Form into three-quarter-inch balls. Bake on ungreased cookie sheet 15 to 20 minutes in a 350 degree oven. While still hot, roll in powdered sugar.

Wedding Rings

- 4 c. flour
- 4 tsp. baking powder
- 1 tbsp. vanilla
- 3 eggs
- 1 c. margarine
- 1 1/2 c. sugar

Mix all ingredients together. Roll out dough to form small circular rings. Bake on an ungreased cookie sheet at 350 degrees for eight to 10 minutes, or until lightly browned. These are usually served plain, but can be iced with a confectioner's sugar icing or glaze.

— JoAnn Thomas

Fudge

- 6 oz. cream cheese
- 4 c. powdered sugar
- 1 tbsp. vanilla
- 1 c. nuts
- 4 oz. bittersweet chocolate, melted

Mix all ingredients. Spread in a lightly buttered dish or drop from spoon on waxed paper. Cool before eating.

— Mary Bednarz

Pickled Herring

- 2 lbs. salt herring
- 2 c. water
- 1/3 c. vinegar
- 1 medium onion, sliced
- 1/4 c. sugar
- 1 tsp. pickling spices
- 1/2 tsp. mustard seed

Skin herring; remove backbone. Cut fish into small, one-to-two-inch pieces. Soak fish in cold water overnight to remove salt.

Drain fish and rinse in cold water. Combine all ingredients and pour over the fish. Marinate overnight in refrigerator. Serve chilled.

Yield: 1 quart.

— Mary Bednarz

Shrimp Curry

- 1 chicken bouilon cube
- 1 c. boiling water
- 5 tbsp. butter or margarine
- 1/2 c. minced onion
- 6 tbsp. flour
- 2 1/2 tsp curry powder
- 1 1/4 tsp. salt
- 1 1/2 tsp. sugar
- 1/4 tsp. powdered ginger
- 2 c. milk
- 4 c. cleaned, cooked shrimp (about 3 lbs. raw)
- 1 tsp. lemon juice

Dissolve bouillon cube in water. Melt butter in top of double boiler and add onion, simmering until tender. Moisten the flour with cold water, making a thick paste, stirring until smooth. Add the paste to the onion mix, stirring well. Add the spices. Gradually stir in the bouillon and milk, cooks over boiling water. Add the shrimp and lemon juice and allow to heat through.

Yield: serves 6.

— Angie DiBella

Polish Potato Salad

- 6 medium potatoes, cooked just tender
- 1/4 c. olive oil
- 1/4 c. vinegar
- 1 tsp. dry mustard powder
- 1 tsp. salt
- 1/2 tsp. ground white pepper
- 1 tbsp. caraway seed
- 1 medium onion, chopped
- 1/2 c. mayonnaise
- 2 hard-boiled eggs, chopped
- 1 tsp. paprika

Slice potatoes into a large bowl. Mix oil, vinegar, mustard, salt, pepper, and caraway seed in a jar. Shake and pour over potatoes. Allow to marinate for one hour. Add onion, salad dressing, chopped eggs, and toss to mix. Place in serving bowl and garnish with paprika.

— Mary Bednarz

Pecan Cheese Logs

- 6 oz. cheddar cheese, grated
- 8 oz. pkg. cream cheese
- 1/2 tbsp. garlic salt
- 3 oz. pecans, finely chopped
- paprika

In a large bowl, soften cheeses. Add garlic salt and pecans, and mix with hands until extremely well blended. Refrigerate until firm again. Roll into large log. Sprinkle paprika generously on waxed paper and roll log in paprika. Dampen hands slightly and roll log between hands until the paprika gives a red coating to the log. Refrigerate until hard. Slice in thin rounds and serve with crackers.

The Funeral Feast

After the death of a loved one, certain rituals are observed. Many of the funeral customs as we know them today are of ancient origin including the funeral feast still common today.

Much honor was early bestowed on the remains of the martyred saints and the places of their burials. Family vaults were small chambers opening from a main corridor. It was here that a memorial feast, or *agape*, took place, corresponding to that held by the pagan Romans in honor of the dead. This meal was probably often preceded or followed by the Eucharist (James, p. 191). The *agape*, sometimes called a "love feast," was to celebrate charity. Saint Paul, in Corinthians 11:20, seems to disapprove of the *agape*, citing rumors of abuse. Eventually, due to abuses, these meals were prohibited and the *agape* disappeared by the eighth century.

As early as the time of St. John Chrysostom, doles of food were made to the poor for thirty days after a funeral. These, plus doles of money, were thought to be beneficial in procuring the repose of the soul of the deceased (James, p. 209).

In the Middle Ages, a feast was always given to the chief mourners in conformity with the ritual of the funeral. Today, gifts of food are often taken to the home of close relatives of the deceased. Families gather after the funeral at the home of the closest relative and a meal is usually shared by all.

When taking gifts of food to a bereaved family, if at all possible, take them in non-returnable containers. Foil over cardboard makes a good plate for a cake or cookies: A foil-lined box will hold meats. Vegetables and salads can be packed in plastic margarine tubs or in glass jars. Or inexpensive plastic dishes may be purchased especially for your gift. If you must use one of your dishes that you wish returned, be certain to write your name on a piece of tape and affix it to your dish to help the family know the proper person to return it to. If the family is a large one, a very thoughtful gift is to supply them with paper goods, including cups, plates, and napkins, and plastic cutlery. If there are a number of relatives from out of town who will be staying with the family, another nice idea is to present the family with breakfast foods such as milk, cereal, eggs, sweet rolls, and the like.

Mama's Meatballs

- 1 lb. ground chuck
- 1 medium onion, chopped finely
- 15 to 20 saltine crackers, crushed
- 1 tsp. garlic powder
- 2 eggs
- 3 tbsp. Worcestershire sauce
- 1 tsp. ground black pepper

- oil to fry
- 1 medium onion, sliced
- 3 c. milk
- 1 tbsp. garlic powder
- 1 tsp. black pepper
- 2 tbsp. cornstarch

Combine first seven ingredients in a bowl. Mix thoroughly with hands. Form into balls. Cover bottom of large skillet with oil. Over medium high heat, brown meatballs, turning to keep round shape and to avoid sticking. When meatballs are nicely browned, pour off excess oil. Add onions. Mix cornstarch in cold milk. Add spices to milk mixture. Pour milk mixture over meatballs. Reduce heat to low. Cover and cook until meat is cooked through. Serve over noodles or rice.

Yield: serves 4 to 6.

Texas-Italian Hominy

- 1/2 lb. ground beef
- 1 tbsp. chopped onion
- 6 oz. sliced pepperoni
- 1/2 c. milk
- 2 slices American cheese, torn into pieces
- 1 tsp. cornstarch

- 1 8 oz. can tomato sauce
- 1/4 tsp. garlic powder
- 1 1/2 tsp. Italian seasoning
- 2 tsp. grated Parmesan cheese
- 2 cans hominy, drained
- 1/2 c. grated Cheddar cheese

Cook ground beef, onion, and pepperoni in small skillet until brown and drain off excess fat. Pour milk into small saucepan and add American cheese. Cook over very hot heat until cheese is melted, stirring constantly. Mix half cup cold water with cornstarch and stir into milk mixture. Cook, stirring until thickened. Add tomato sauce, seasonings, Parmesan cheese, and mix well. Pour hominy into a two-qt. casserole and add meat mixture. Pour sauce over mix and sprinkle Cheddar cheese on top. Bake in preheated 350 degree oven 15 minutes or until heated through.

Yield: serves 4 to 6.

Cornbread Salad

- 1 pan cornbread, crumbled
- 8 slices crisp bacon, crumbled
- 1 large onion, chopped fine
- 1 bell pepper, chopped
- 1 or two medium tomatoes, chopped
- 1 pint mayonnaise
- 1 small can whole kernel corn, drained

Mix all ingredients. Add salt and pepper to taste. Refrigerate for at least an hour before serving. Yield: 1 salad.

— Adilene Douglas

Shirl's Spinach

- 1 10 oz. pkg. frozen chopped spinach, cooked by package directions
- 3 tbsp. freshly grated Parmesan cheese
- 3 tbsp. chopped onion
- 3 tbsp. evaporated milk
- 3 tbsp. margarine, melted
- crushed round buttery crackers

Add cheese, onion and milk to spinach. Stir to combine and place in a one-qt. buttered casserole. Top with cracker crumbs and margarine. Bake at 350 degrees about five to ten minutes.
Yield: serves 4.

— Shirl Gallagher

Coconut Butter Cream Cake

- 1 Duncan Hines butter cake mix, baked according to package directions, but in two layers instead of three
- 10 oz. Cool Whip
- 8 oz. sour cream
- 2 c. sugar
- 1 tsp. vanilla
- shredded or flaked coconut

Using a strong sewing thread, circle each layer and by pulling thread crosswise cut each layer in half. You will have four layers.

Stir together all other ingredients except coconut. Cover the top of each layer and sprinkle on coconut as you stack the layers. Use remainder of icing to spread on outside of cake.

Yield: 1 four-layer cake.

— Adilene Douglas

Buttermilk Pie

- 1 stick margarine
- 2 c. sugar
- 3 tbsp. (rounded) flour
- 3 slightly beaten eggs
- 1 c. buttermilk
- 2 tsp. vanilla

In some parts of the United States, this pie was also known as a "shoofly" pie.

Mix all ingredients well and pour into an unbaked pie shell. This will be a thin batter with little lumps of margarine floating in it. Bake at 350 degrees for 55 minutes or until knife inserted in center comes out clean. The top of the pie will be crusty with a smooth under-filling.

Coke Cake

- 2 c. flour
- 2 c. sugar
- 2 sticks margarine
- 3 tbsp. cocoa
- 1 c. dark cola
- 1/2 c. buttermilk
- 2 beaten eggs
- 1 tsp. soda
- 1 tsp. vanilla
- 1 1/2 c. miniature marshmallows

Combine flour and sugar. Heat butter, cocoa, and cola to boiling and pour flour-sugar mix over it. Mix thoroughly. Add buttermilk, eggs, soda, and vanilla. Add marshmallows. Beat together and mix well. This will be a thin batter with marshmallows floating on top. Bake in large glass baking dish at 350 degrees for 30 to 35 minutes. Ice while hot.

Icing:

- 1/2 c. butter
- 3 tbsp. cocoa
- 6 tbsp. dark cola drink
- 1 box powdered sugar
- 1 c. chopped, toasted nuts

Combine butter, cocoa, and cola and heat to boiling. Pour over powdered sugar. Beat well and add nuts. Spread on hot cake.

Taco Soup

- 2 lbs. ground meat
- 1 onion — chopped fine
- 1 pkg taco mix
- 1 pkg Ranch style buttermilk dressing mix
- 1 tsp. garlic powder
- 2 cans whole tomatoes, chopped into pieces, plus juice
- 1 can yellow hominy, drained
- 1 small can chopped green chilies
- 1 can plain pinto beans
- 1 can Ranch Style beans
- 2 c. water

Brown the meat and onion. Drain off excess grease. In a large pan, place meat mixture, garlic powder, taco mix and buttermilk dressing mix. Stir well. Add remaining ingredients. Simmer 30 minutes. Add more water if needed. Serve with cornbread for a complete meal.

Yield: serves 10 to 12.

— Gracine Griffin

Blueberry Salad

- 1 large can blueberry pie filling
- 1 can crushed pineapple (15 1/2 oz.) — do not drain
- 1 6 oz. pkg. raspberry jello
- 2 c. boiling water
- 8 oz. pkg. cream cheese
- 1/2 c. sugar
- 8 oz. sour cream
- 1 tsp. vanilla
- 1 c. chopped nuts

Mix together the first four ingredients thoroughly, place in serving bowl and chill. Make topping by mixing the last five ingredients. When base is thoroughly chilled and set, spread on topping and store in refrigerator until time to serve.

Yield: serves 8 to 10.

— Gracine Griffin

What Jesus Ate

We do not, of course, have records of the exact foods that Jesus ate. However, archeologists have discovered much about the life and times of the people in the days when Christ walked on earth. It is a safe assumption that Jesus would have followed the customs, including the food customs, of the Jews who lived in His day.

The Blessed Mother would have baked the bread for her family, once a week, at the village bakehouse. (Neither bakeries nor stables were allowed under dwelling houses.) The village women took turns baking their bread. Inside the bakehouse was an earthen oven about three feet round and five feet long, sunk in the ground. The fire was made by burning thorn and straw. One to two hundred loaves could be baked at one time. This would be one week's baking, for each loaf was thin and three loaves made a meal for a single person. Mary would prepare the dough and mix in the leaven in the morning. After the bread fermented all morning, she would go to the bakehouse in the afternoon. Jesus might have gone with His mother and kept busy feeding the fire. The walls of the hut were black with soot, and the bakers often had to rush out into the open air, away from the choking smoke.

Sometimes, instead of taking bread to the bakehouse, Mary would make flat cakes and roast them over glowing embers in her charcoal fire or on a flat iron plate at home.

Each morning before school, Jesus helped His mother to grind some corn; a little must be ground every day, for they were using a hand-mill and it was slow work.

On the eve of the sabbath, Mary cleaned and prepared the house. A table was placed in front of the piled-up sleeping mattresses. The pre-sabbath meal would have a meat dish, instead of the usual bread, vegetables, rice, milk, and honey. No one could go without on the Sabbath; those who were better off gave to the very poor, and Mary and Jesus would have taken food to a poor family in the early morning.

When Joseph returned from the Synagogue, he would bring guests with him. Mary and Jesus would hand around water and towels, so that hands and feet could be washed before sitting or reclining on the mattresses and beginning the meal. They would sup at five. There were no forks or spoons; the meat was cut up with a knife and they would eat with their fingers or dip strips of bread into the broth (Boulting, p. 104).

Luke tells us that when Jesus was twelve years old, He went to Jerusalem with His parents to attend the Passover, the feast that celebrated the deliverance of Israel from Egyptian bondage hundreds of years before. A paschal lamb was ceremoniously slain and blessed by the priests at the temple. Ten to twenty persons formed a supper-party, and a lamb was sacrificed and eaten by each party.

After services at the Temple, Joseph and Jesus would return to their supper-party. The lamb had been roasted on a spit of pomegranate wood. When all had settled themselves, reclining on the ground, the meal would begin. The leader would fill a cup with wine while repeating a blessing; he would pass it round and all would drink from it. After this there was a general washing of hands; the leader would dip bitter herbs, called marror, in salt water, eat of it himself, and give it to the others.

As dishes were removed, the cup was refilled, and the youngest present (Jesus) would ask: "What mean you by this feast?" The eldest of the company would reply, "It is the sacrifice of the Lord's passover, who passed over the houses of the children of Israel and delivered our houses."

Now the dishes were returned again; the leader lifted the dish of lamb, then the herbs, and then the bread, explaining the symbolic meaning of each. The lamb represented God's passing, the unleavened bread the delivery in haste from Egypt, and the herbs the bitterness of their forefathers' lives in Egypt. Next psalms were sung, the bread was broken into pieces, thanks were given, and the pieces were dipped together with the herbs in a mixture of raisins, dates and vinegar called *charoseth* (or *haroset*). The reddish color of this food recalled the mortar and bricks the slaves had been forced to make in Egypt. Then the lamb was eaten, a third cup of wine drunk, over which a special blessing was spoken, and finally a fourth cup of wine taken during the singing of psalms of praise (Boulting, pp. 186-207).

Today's Jews observe Passover much as Jesus did in His time. The holiday is observed for eight days in the United States. Unleavened bread is usually eaten during this spring holiday. A waferlike pastry called matzo is one of the best known Passover foods. Cakes, cookies, and dumplings for Passover are made from either potato starch or matzo meal, made from ground matzos. Other traditional foods for Passover include gefilte fish, chicken soup, and roast chicken. Because Jews scattered throughout much of the world, different communities have developed varying interpretations of the Passover laws, so foods for the Passover table vary. After tasting the ritual foods and drinking wine in the order explained in a special book of procedures and prayers, the Passover dinner itself begins.

Many Catholic churches have developed the custom in recent years of holding a Passover Seder to show in a concrete way a bit of the lifestyle of Jesus. Sometimes churches cooperate with a local synagogue in presenting such a meal for the entire parish. Sometimes groups within the parish hold small observances. My own parish, Corpus Christi, hosts a seder served by the catechumens.

Fig Preserves

• 3 qt. figs   • 9 c. sugar

Wash figs, do not remove stems. Place in large boiler with sugar. Start on low heat and bring to boil. Cook until figs are done, but not too soft or mushy. Remove figs from pan with slotted spoon and continue cooking juice until it thickens, about 15 minutes. Return figs to syrup. Heat thoroughly and pour immediately into hot sterilized jars. Seal. A thin slice of lemon may be added to each jar.

— Glen Burleson

Lite Chicken Soup

- 1 fryer, cut in pieces
- 9 c. cold water
- 1 large onion, peeled and chopped
- 1 large carrot, peeled and chopped
- 2 celery stalks, including leafy tops, chopped
- 5 sprigs parsley, chopped
- 1/4 c. frozen English peas
- salt and pepper
- 1 tbsp. margarine
- 1 tbsp. cornstarch

Bake chicken in 350-degree oven until done, approximately 35 to 45 minutes. Cool. De-bone, and dispose of skin and bones. Dissolve cornstarch in a cup of the water. Place all ingredients in a large pan and bring to a boil. Reduce heat and simmer 20 to 30 minutes. Ladle into bowls and add drained matzo balls.

Yield: serves 6 to 8.

Matzo Balls

- 2 eggs
- 1 tbsp. oil
- 1/2 c. matzo meal
- 1/2 tsp. salt
- pinch of ginger
- 2 tbsp. water

Beat eggs with oil in a medium mixing bowl. Add meal, salt, and ginger, stirring until well-blended. Stir in water. Let mixture stand for 20 minutes until meal absorbs liquid.

Bring two quarts salted water to a boil in a large saucepan. With wet hands, take about 1 tsp. of matzo-ball mixture and roll it between your palms into a ball; mixture will be soft. Set balls on a plate. With a rubber spatula, carefully slide balls into boiling water. Cover and simmer over low heat about 30 minutes or until firm. Keep warm and covered until ready to serve. They can be made ahead and kept covered, in their cooking liquid, in refrigerator. Reheat gently in cooking liquid or in soup before serving. Serve drained balls in chicken soup.

Haroset

- 1 medium orange
- 10 pitted dates
- 1/2 c. slivered almonds
- 1 large apple, peeled, cored, and cut into large pieces
- 1 or 2 small bananas

- 1 tbsp. lemon juice
- 1 tbsp. sugar
- 1 tsp. ground cinnamon
- 1/4 c. sweet red wine
- 1/3 c. matzo meal

Use a grater to remove most of the colored part of the orange. Reserve the grated rind. Finish peeling, section, and cut the orange into pieces. Finely grind the orange rind, orange pieces, dates, almonds, apple, and banana. Stir in the lemon juice, sugar, cinnamon, and wine. Add enough of the matzo meal for the desired consistency. The mixture will get a little thicker as it sits. Refrigerate the haroset in a covered container and serve chilled. It will keep fresh for about two days in the refrigerator.

The *Agape* Meal

No fact of the Gospel history is better attested than that Jesus held a farewell supper with His disciples. The incident is narrated in all three Synoptic Gospels, plus 1 Corinthians 11:23-26, where Paul explicitly says he has received the account from the church before him. It seems to have been Jesus' custom to close the day with a meal in company with His followers, and after His death they continued the practice which recalled Him to them vividly, and they now observed the meal with a special memory of His last supper. Thus, the "breaking of bread," was a custom of the church from the earliest days. At first the Eucharist was connected with the *agape*, the common meal by which the believers signalized their brotherhood, but the combination of the ordinary meal with the sacred one was eventually discontinued, probably because of such abuses as Paul condemns in 1 Corinthians 11:20-22.

The *agape* was a fraternal banquet celebrated by the early Christians as a symbol of their mutual charity and union in one family. The practice of holding such common meals, or "love feasts," seems to have been borrowed from pagan custom. A sacramental meal was a familiar feature of many ancient religions. At first, the *agape* preceded the eucharistic celebration, and the interval was filled with readings from Scripture, prayers, and the singing of psalms. Toward the beginning of the second century, the *agape* was separated from the Mass, which was normally celebrated in the morning while the agape took place in the evening and it was seldom celebrated on Sunday.

The *agape* was held in private homes or in churches, with a bishop, presbyter, or deacon presiding. According to Hippolytus, the host provided the meal, invited the guests, including the poor and needy, and expected the guests to pray for him in return. From Tertullian we learn that the meal was begun and ended with prayer. After eating, each one present sang a hymn or psalm and possibly prophesied.

The *agape* was supposed to promote Christian fellowship and love and to unite those participating in closer relationship with Christ, who was considered to be the unseen head of the table. Increasingly the meal became a charity supper or a memorial to the departed. When the faithful began to multiply, it became increasingly difficult to arrange these affairs, and abuses such as drunkenness and gluttony crept in. By the eighth century, these "love feasts" had practically disappeared. In modern times, the agape in one form or another was revived by the Moravians, Mennonites, Dunkards, Methodists, and some other sects. A remnant of the *agape* is found in the Cursillo movement.

We do not know exactly what these early Christians ate at their *agape* meal, although some biblical texts refer to wine having been served (and consumed in excess; cf. 1 Cor. 11:17-34; Jude 12). Through archeological research, we do know the foods that were grown and available to the early Christians as well as the shapes of some of the cooking utensils and methods of cooking used.

There are no exact recipes as we know them today from the earliest centuries. Gavius Apicius, who lived in the first century, wrote the earliest cookbook still extant. Using his directions and our knowledge of foods available, we can imagine the types of food these early Christians may have eaten, and can create our own recipes. In this manner, we can experience a crossing of the time barrier to a closeness with our early Christian ancestors.

We can adopt the concept of *agape* and serve a meal to our family and friends based on Christian fellowship and love. Children love ceremony and would enjoy helping to prepare a meal based on foods available to Jesus' first friends. The head of the family can say special prayers of thanksgiving and love to begin the *agape*, and each member present can be encouraged to add a personal prayer.

Below is a discussion of the most common foods available to early Christians. For your own *agape,* create a menu using these foods, or try our recipes which follow.

Common fruits were apricots, figs, dates, pomegranates, quince, watermelons, muskmelons, cucumbers, and olives. Nuts included walnut, pistachio, almond, and pine nuts. For variety, there were citron and carob. Lentils and broad (fava) beans were welcome vegetables in the daily pottage. A variety of grains were used for bread, including wheat, millet, and barley. There was no corn such as we know it from the Indian maize; the corn referred to in the bible was a vegetable mixture which included beans, lentils, barley and cumin. Kernels of wheat and barley just harvested might be roasted to become "parched corn."

Along with leeks and onions, there were other salad foods often referred to as "bitter herbs." These were most probably chicory, sorrel, watercress, lettuce, and dandelion. These leaves were enjoyed raw in salads or cooked in soups or stews. Sometimes the green potherbs were blended with mustard. Watercress, mint, and possibly endive were also eaten as potherbs.

Although pumpkin, winter squash, and crookneck are all cultivated in the Holy Land today, the members of the squash family as we know them were natives of the New World. Some researchers believe, however, that a wild ancestor of one of these was the mysterious gourd mentioned in the Bible. Some wild ancestors of other vegetables were definitely available by the early Christian era. The thistle was cultivated to become our artichoke, and the mallow was probably a forerunner of today's spinach.

The tops of carrots were at first the only part of the vegetable considered fit to eat. There is a first-century recipe for frying carrots and parsnips and serving them with a dressing.

Breadmaking was a well-established profession by the time of the first Christians. Their ordinary loaf of bread was round; it varied in thickness. Unleavened bread was called matzah or matzo. It was just such bread that the Hebrews had cooked in haste on the night of their escape with Moses, and even today at Passover the Jews use this bread. Usually, however, bread was allowed to rise. A small lump of dough from the previous day's baking was added as a "starter" to the new dough. Bread was served in light wicker baskets, and the head of the household broke the bread and gave it to the rest of the family and to guests. Bits of this bread were used almost as we use spoons to scoop the hot food from the communal bowl.

Milk was usually stored in goatskins. Often, it fermented into "leben," our modern-day yogurt. Butter was churned by rocking the skins back and forth, but because of the hot climate it quickly became rancid unless it was boiled. This was called "samn," which we know today as clarified butter. Honey and syrups made from fruit were the most common sweeteners of the day; sugar was imported only for the table of the very wealthy.

Fish played an important role in the diet of the early Christians. The Sea of Galilee teemed with many varieties of fish; salted, dried, and smoked fish were imported. The fish was chosen as one of the earliest of Christian symbols. The first Christians who did not dare to publicly admit their faith recognized each other by the drawings of the fish emblem. The name of Jesus was represented in the form of a fish because the first five letters of the word "fish" in Greek stood for the first letters of words which stated their belief: "Jesus Christ, God's Son, Savior."

Quail, partridge, pheasant, duck, goose, pigeon, dove, and, for the very rich, peacocks, were popular table fowl. The most common fowl, just as today, was the domestic chicken. Goats and sheep were the primary meat animals, although rarely a cow or ox may have been roasted for a special feast. A number of varieties of deer and antelope were plentiful. Although forbidden to the Hebrews by Mosaic law, wild hare and boar may both have been enjoyed by the early Christians.

Beverages included a variety of fruit drinks and teas made from steeping herbs and spices. Grapes were pressed for juice and fermented for wine.

Herbs and spices grew well in the sun-drenched holy land. Favorites of the early Christian era included anise, caraway, coriander, cumin, dill, fennel, hyssop (savory), mint, mustard, parsley, rue, saffron, sage, marjoram, and thyme.

Stuffed Grape Leaves

- 1/2 c. rice
- 1 small onion, minced
- 1/4 c. parsley, chopped fine
- 1/4 c. mint leaves, chopped fine
- 1 egg, beaten
- 1/4 tsp. pepper, freshly ground
- 1 lb. ground lamb (or beef), browned with fat drained off
- 1 3/4 tsp. salt
- 4 doz. grape leaves (or substitute romaine leaves)
- 2 c. beef or chicken bouillon (or stock)
- 2 tbsp. margarine

Broccoli is an ancient vegetable. In the second century, the Romans grew and loved the same kind of sprouting broccoli we eat today.

Combine the first seven ingredients with 3/4 tsp. salt, mixing well. Place a rounded teaspoon of mixture in the center of each leaf, fold in sides and roll up. Stack, side by side and in layers, in a three-quart saucepan. Add the stock, margarine, and remaining salt. Put a heat-proof plate inside the saucepan with a weight on it to hold the grape leaves down. Cover and simmer for 45 minutes. Place leaves on a serving dish to serve as appetizers. If desired, thicken the leftover stock with a little flour or cornstarch and pour over the grape leaves. These are also good served cold.

If you do not grow your own grapes, wild grapes grow in many parts of the United States. Check with your local arboretum or public librarian as to how to locate and identify these vines. Caution: although wild grapes make wonderful jellies and preserves, they are not suitable for eating straight off the vine. They have a bitter substance that can blister sensitive mouths.

To prepare fresh grape leaves: rinse thoroughly. Stack in a kettle and cover with boiling water. Boil for 1 minute with 1/2 tsp. salt. Leaves will turn to an olive green. Drain. Bottled leaves, available in Middle Eastern specialty stores, should be drained and soaked in cold water for 15 minutes to remove salt. Boil for 1 minute with fresh water before using. Drain.

Yield: about 4 dozen.

Cucumeres

- 1 large cucumber, peeled and sliced
- 1/2 c. boiling water
- 1 beef bouillon cube
- 1/2 c. vinegar
- 3 tbsp. honey
- 1/2 tsp. ground white pepper
- 1/2 tsp. ground pennyroyal (or substitute mint)

Dissolve bouillon cube in boiling water, place in a bowl with the vinegar, honey and spices. Add cucumber slices. Chill for at least an hour before serving.

Yield: serves 2 to 4.

— adapted from Apicius

Vegetable Fritters

- 1 large yellow squash
- 1/2 onion
- 1 carrot
- 1 c. flour
- 1 egg
- 1/2 c. milk
- 1 tbsp. oil
- 1 tsp. lemon pepper
- 1 tsp. salt
- 1 tsp. garlic powder
- 1 tbsp. chopped fresh parsley (or substitute dried flakes)
- 2 fresh basil leaves, chopped (or substitute dried basil)

Mix flour, egg, milk, oil, and spices. Add chopped vegetables. Drop by large spoonfuls into skillet of hot oil and fry until golden brown. Drain on brown paper or paper towel and salt to taste.

Baked Fish Fillets

- 2 lbs. fish fillets
- 1 can golden cream of mushroom soup
- 1/2 soup can water
- 1 tsp. thyme
- 1 tsp. lemon pepper
- 1/2 tsp. salt
- sprinkle of paprika

Place filets in a lightly oiled oven-proof dish. Mix the other ingredients, except paprika, and stir until smooth. Pour mixture over filets. Sprinkle top with paprika. Bake in a preheated 350-degree oven until fish is tender — eight to 10 minutes may be enough.

Yield: serves 4 to 6.

Agape Stew

- 1 1/2 lbs. ground meat*
- 1/2 medium onion, chopped
- 1 1/2 c. water
- 1 heaping tbsp. cornstarch
- 1 tsp. garlic powder
- 1 tsp. oregano
- 1 tsp. salt
- 1 tsp. coarse ground black pepper
- 2 tsp. ground cumin

Brown meat and drain off fat. Add onions and cook until clear. Dissolve cornstarch in the water and add to mixture, cooking and stirring until mixture thickens. Add spices. Serve hot with toast triangles or with buttered noodles or rice.

We prefer ground chuck, but any type of ground meat will work.

Honey Sesame Crisps

- 2 c. flour
- 1/2 tsp. salt
- 1/4 c. honey
- 1/2 c. warm water

- extra honey
- pkg. sesame seeds

Stir together the 1/4 c. honey and water to melt honey. Add the other ingredients to make a dough that can be gathered into a ball. On a lightly floured surface, turn out dough and knead for ten minutes. Divide into 12 even pieces, roll into balls. Roll out into thin, four-inch discs.

Lightly brush the tops of discs with honey. Sprinkle with sesame seed.

Bake on an ungreased cookie sheet in a preheated 500-degree oven for five minutes or until discs are lightly colored, blistered, and crisp. Serve with cheese, fruit, dips or soup.

Yield: 1 dozen 4-inch crisps.

Honeyed Nuts

- 1 c. shelled nuts
- 1/2 c. sugar

- 1 tbsp. honey

Toast the nuts in a 350-degree oven for about ten minutes. Heat the sugar, stirring constantly, in a small skillet over low heat until it begins to melt and caramelize. Blend in the honey. Stir in the nuts. Remove from heat and immediately drop into clusters onto a lightly greased baking sheet.

Just for Fun

In my raggedy recipe file. I have a number of recipes that I keep because they amuse me or because they are not so much recipes as chemical compositions. For some, I simply can't think of a better place to keep them until I need them. Perhaps you can use these off-beat recipes to make something fun, or beautiful, or functional.

Scripture Cake

- 1 c. butter (Judges 5:25: milk)
- 2 c. sugar (Jeremiah 6:20: sweet cane)
- 3 1/2 c. flour (1 Kings 5:2: Solomon's provisions)
- 2 c. figs (1 Samuel 30:12: cake of pressed figs)
- 2 c. raisins ("   " : two clusters of raisins)
- 1 c. water (Genesis 24:22: drinking by camels)
- 1 c. almonds (Genesis 43:11: almonds)
- 6 eggs (Isaiah 10:14: as one gathers eggs)
- 1/4 tsp. salt (Leviticus 5:13: every meal seasoned)
- 2 tbsp. honey (Exodus 16:14: manna, like wafers, honey)
- 1 tsp. cinnamon (1 Kings 10:2: Sheba came with spices)
- 1/4 tsp. allspice
- 1/4 tsp. mace
- 1/4 tsp. ginger
- Follow Solomon's advice for making good boys: Beat well (Proverbs 23:14)

Cream butter and sugar. Stir in half the amount of sifted flour. Chop figs and raisins in a cup of hot water. Blanch, chop, and add the almonds. Beat egg yolks and stir in honey. Beat egg whites with a pinch of salt until they stand in peaks. Combine yolks and honey alternately with remaining flour sifted with salt and spices. Stir in egg whites. Beat slightly. Put batter in a large rectangular pan lined with wax paper. Bake at 375 degrees about 50 minutes or until cake is browned on top and begins to pull away from sides of pan. Cool, cut into squares.

This cake was contributed to a New England church fair contest by some unknown little Yankee girl who obviously knew her Bible well (McLaughlin, p. 244).

Barriga de Freira (Nun's Belly)

- 1/2 c. sugar
- 1/2 c. water
- 2 tbsp. butter or margarine
- 8 slices of white bread, torn
- 4 egg yolks, beaten
- cinnamon to taste

In a saucepan, combine the sugar and water and boil for a few minutes to make a syrup. Remove the pan from the heat and add the butter. Stir until it has melted into the syrup. Tear the bread into tiny pieces. Add the bread to the syrup, mixing thoroughly. Put the pan over low heat and gradually stir in the beaten egg yolks. Cook, stirring, just until the eggs thicken the mixture and are cooked. Pour the mixture into a small serving dish about 4" x 6" x 1". Sprinkle cinnamon on top. Decorate with nuts or crystallized fruit if you wish. Refrigerate. Serve in small squares on chilled plates.

Yield: four small portions.

Portuguese nuns created many delicious sweet things in the sixteenth and seventeenth centuries. Sugar plantations in the New World had made sugar cheap and available for the first time in Europe's history, and eggs were plentiful. Additionally, there was the Moorish influence of rich sweets. The nuns sold their sweet things to raise money for their convents. The sixteenth century was also a time when very strange names were given to foods. Some of our favorites are Old Clothes, Angel's Breasts, and Nun's Belly (Ortiz, p. 89).

Blue Food Salad

- 1 can pear halves, drained
- 4 oz. pkg. cream cheese
- 6 lettuce leaves
- 1/4 c. blanched almonds, chopped fine
- cake color

Soften cheese and mix with almonds and a few drops of blue cake color. Fill cavity in each pear with cheese mixture and arrange on a serving plate on a bed of lettuce. Chill before serving.

Yield: serves 6.

This salad was my first effort at serving Blue Food. It has since become a classic at my house.

Chemical Garden

- 1/4 c. salt
- 1/4 c. blueing
- 1/4 c. ammonia
- charcoal briquets or charcoal

Break briquets into irregular pieces. Place in glass container. Pour solution over it. A chemical garden will begin to grow in a few hours. From time to time, add salt. Cake color will add color to the garden. Place a tiny manger scene or statue in center of garden.

Dough Art

- 2 c. all-purpose flour
- 1 c. salt
- 1 c. water

In medium mixing bowl, mix flour and salt. Gradually add water, stirring until mixture forms a ball. Knead on floured surface for 7 to 10 minutes, or until dough is smooth.

Use the dough as you would clay. You can roll it to 1/4" thickness and cut with cookie cutters for ornaments or hand shape miniatures. To attach two pieces of dough, moisten with water and pinch. All shapes should be less than 1/2" thick for best results.

Lightly spray a microwaveable baking sheet or plate with vegetable cooking spray. Microwave on high power for several minutes, until dough is firm and almost dry. (Or place in slow oven for several minutes.) Transfer to wire rack and let your project dry at least 24 hours before decorating.

You can paint ornaments with acrylic paints or use markers to color dried shapes. A soda straw will punch neat holes for ornaments, but holes need to be made before microwaving. Magnets can be attached to miniatures. Finish by spraying with several coats of clear acrylic spray. Sprinkle wet coating with glitter if desired.

This clay is useful for making Christmas ornaments. It can be stored in a plastic bag for about two days.

Homemade Lye Soap

- 1 can lye
- 2 1/2 pints cold water
- 6 lbs. clean fat (such as bacon grease, but it must not be burned)

Today's chick peas are the esteemed "pulse" of the Hebrews and Egyptians.

Slowly add lye to cold water, stir until dissolved. Never use glass, stoneware, or aluminum vessels. Melt fat. Let cool to lukewarm. Pour lye solution into melted fat in a thin steady stream while steadily stirring. Takes about 10 to 20 minutes. It will become thick as honey. Pour this into a cardboard box. Let stand 24 hours. Remove and cut into bars. Keep in a cool dry place. Note: LYE IS DANGEROUS! This project is best made outside, but if you make it inside, make certain you have proper ventilation.

Making this soap can give you a better appreciation of our pioneer forefathers. Additionally, it is a good way to recycle your meat fat.

Fireplace Fantasy

- 4 lbs. copper sulfate
- 3 lbs. ice cream salt
- 5 gallons water

Your homemade Yule log will sparkle and flame in brilliant colors. This is also a welcome and unique gift for friends with fireplaces. Warning: This mixture is toxic and extremely caustic. Use caution and keep out of way of children and pets.

In a large crock (do not use any metal container), mix ingredients above.

Wrap newspapers into tight logs, tying with string. (Or treat pinecones with solution.) Soak newspapers in mixture until they are well soaked. Place to dry on a concrete floor or in a safe spot on paper on dirt. When logs are thoroughly dry, wrap them in colored tissue paper, tying ends with paper ribbon or with string.

Fund-raisers

Each time I attend Mass in my hometown of Jacksonville, Texas, I smile at the thought of a church built on pasta.

When I was a child, the Catholic community in this part of Texas was small; it was mission territory for the sturdy LaSallette Fathers who served there. In the late 1950s, the priest traveled well over a hundred miles each Sunday, saying Mass in a number of small towns. The church in Jacksonville was a simple wooden building. The parishioners wanted a real church, something beautiful for God. So they cooked.

Annually, the local Catholics presented a spaghetti supper to which the entire community was invited. The dinners were held in the local hotel, and my parents always bought tickets.

In addition to food, there were raffles and other activities. My favorite was the post office. For a small sum of money, you could purchase a box, in standard brown wrapping paper, which had been mailed to the local church from Catholics all over the United States. Who knew what wonderful surprise would be in the package you picked? The boxes were in all shapes and sizes, and it was fun to shake and feel as many as you could before the next child in line poked you in the back with a whispered "Hurry up, don't take all day!" I still have a small ceramic horned toad bought at one of these annual events.

Eventually enough pasta was prepared and sold, along with donations and other funds, to build Our Lady of Sorrows Catholic church.

The recipes that follow were used in the fund-raisers which built this church. The pasta was accompanied by a green salad and garlic bread.

One Cooker Chicken Spaghetti

- 2 hens or 1/2 turkey
- 2 stalks celery, chopped
- 4 onions, chopped
- 3 cans tomatoes
- 2 cans Cream of mushroom soup
- 3 1 lb. packages spaghetti

- 3 bell peppers, chopped
- 1/2 lb. margarine or butter
- 1 1/2 lbs. Velveeta cheese
- 3 garlic cloves, crushed, or 1/2 tsp. garlic powder
- salt and pepper to taste

Boil and de-bone chicken and chill. Melt margarine in cooker at 500 degrees. Add onions, celery, bell pepper, and garlic. Cook until tender. Add tomatoes, chicken, and soup. Cook spaghetti in boiling water until half done, then drain. Add spaghetti (and broth if dry). Grate cheese over and stir in the last 30 minutes.

Note: Do not add spaghetti until last possible chance, as it will not remain firm but will cook to pieces if added too soon. This works up fast if you have everything chopped and ready beforehand. Cook spaghetti in 1 1/2 qts. water or 1 1/2 c. chicken broth. If using turkey, add 2 buttons garlic, 1 whole onion, and the celery leaves to the water in which you boil the turkey. Reserve broth and cut turkey in bite-size pieces.

Yield: serves 50.

— Lillian Moffeit

Shellroni

- 3 lbs. ground meat
- 1 #2 can tomatoes
- 2 large onions, chopped
- 2 cloves garlic, chopped
- 1 small can tomato sauce
- 1 can mushroom soup
- 1/2 lb. cheese
- 1 small can mushroom buttons, drained
- 6 slices bacon
- salt to taste
- 1 1/2 to 2 c. macaroni shells
- 2 1/2 c. water

Fry bacon and drain. Cook ground meat and add drained bacon. Add tomatoes, onions, garlic, tomato sauce, mushroom soup, mushrooms, and water. Simmer 1 1/2 hours. Cool and skim off excess fat. Reheat with partially cooked macaroni shells. Add cheese and cook until cheese melts.

— Lillian Moffeit

Appendixes

Sources
Thank You
Bibliography

Sources

In this book, I have tried to use items and ingredients that would be easily available in most cities of the United States. In some parts of the country, however, some items may not be easily located. The addresses below may help to provide sources for some of these items.

Oplatek, the Polish Christmas wafer, may be ordered from: Franciscan Friars of the Assumption Province, Pulaski, WI 54162. There is no set price, but the order does request a donation to support the work of their province.

Tamales, the Mexican Christmas savories are detailed in a number of good cookbooks. One interesting one we like the best is *The South Texas Mexican Cookbook* by Lucy Garza. You can order this book from Eakin Press, P.O. 90159 Austin, TX 78709. The cost as of this writing is $11.45, postage included. Tamales may also be found in the Mexican food section of your local grocery store in cans or in the frozen food department.

Herbs and Spices. A Moveable Feast, 2202 West Alabama, Houston, TX 77098, has a large selection of herbs and spices which may be ordered by the ounce or by the pound. If you cannot locate a particular spice in your area of the country, you may call or write to them to see if they carry it. Their phone is (713)528-3585.

Specialty Produce. Frieda's Specialty Produce has many produce specialties that may be mail-ordered. The company offers an interesting catalog and recipes that use the unusual produce. Frieda's Inc., P.O. Box 58488, Los Angeles, CA 90058. (800)421-9477.

Allergy-Restricted Specialties. Ener-G Foods, Inc., offers an extensive product line of foods for those on allergy-restricted diets. People with severe allergies can substitute baking mixes, gluten-free pasta, milk substitutes, and a variety of other ingredients to enjoy most of the recipes in this book. Write for information about their product line to Ener-G Foods, Inc., P.O. Box 84487, Seattle, WA 98124-5787, or call (800) 331-5222.

Thank You

Thanks to all whose enthusiasm for this project and whose prayers, recipes, and encouragement have made it possible. If I have inadvertently omitted to thank anyone who helped on this project. I leave it to Our Blessed Mother to extend my thanks and apologies.

Betsy Altenburger, Houston, Texas
Joanna Ball, Frankfort, Germany
Sam and Danielle Ball, San Francisco, California

Mary Bednarz, Buffalo, New York

Rev. Matthew Berko, Chancellor, Ukrainian Catholic Diocese of Stamford, Connecticut

Rev. John Boscoe. C.S.B., Sugarland, Texas

Jim Brennan, Houston, Texas

Lee Brown, Houston, Texas

Verna Burke, San Antonio, Texas

Glen Burleson, Houston, Texas

Sister Mary Carita, Convent Station, New Jersey

Carmen Chapa, Alice, Texas

Andrew Chuba, Wilkes-Barre, Pennsylvania

Roland Contreras, Houston, Texas

Joan Cruz, New Orleans, Louisiana

Charles Davenport, Adelphi, Maryland

Adilene Douglas, Jacksonville, Texas

Julie Douglas, Jacksonville, Texas

Rabbi Stuart Federow, Houston, Texas

Shirl Gallagher, Houston, Texas

Rev. James Gaunt, Sugarland, Texas

Dr. Abe Goldfarb, Jacksonville, Texas

Fred Goporo, Pensacola Jr. College, Pensacola, Florida

Gracine Griffin, Jacksonville, Texas

Mike and Chasie Grisaffe, Houston, Texas

Andrew Harrison, Houston, Texas

JoAnn Hawkins, Ellicott City, Maryland

Tricia Hempel, Catholic Telegraph, Cincinnati, Ohio

Heather Horn, Houston, Texas

Lonnie Hortick, Catholic Bulletin Board, Austin, Texas

Rev. Msgr. Michael J. Kail, Our Lady of the Cedars of Mt. Lebanon Maronite Catholic Church, Fairlawn, Ohio

Lillian Kaiser, Chimney Sweep Books, Santa Cruz, California

Carolyn Kares, Houston, Texas

Mildred Kerr, Houston, Texas

Leo Knowles, Manchester, England

Rev. Charles Kovari, S.J., St. Laudislaus Church, Courtland, Ontario, Canada

John Laughlin, Our Sunday Visitor, Huntington, Indiana

Sister Laurence, O.S.B.M., Secretary, Ukrainian Catholic Diocese of St. Josaphat in Parma, Parma, Ohio

Maryanne Lawless, Los Altos, California

Diana Littlefield, Houston, Texas

Most Rev. Innocent Lotocky, O.S.B.M., Bishop of St. Nicholas in Chicago for Ukrainians, Chicago, Illinois

Mrs. Miklos Majorcsak, Tillsonbury, Ontario, Canada

Consuela "Mache" Martinez, Corpus Christi, Texas

John McAleer, Boston College, Boston, Massachusetts

Margaret McDougle, Jacksonville, Texas

Isabella Medina, Rosenberg, Texas

Lillian Moffeit, Our Lady of Sorrows Catholic Church, Jacksonville, Texas

Ann Molinaro, Houston, Texas

Elizabeth Moore, Covington, Louisiana

Jackie Murphy, *Our Sunday Visitor*, Huntington, Indiana

Karin Murthough, Houston, Texas
Virginia Murthough, Houston, Texas
Joan Neubauer, Houston, Texas
Helen Nixon, Houston, Texas
Sister Helena Paskevich. S.S.M.S., Sloatsburg, New York
Most Rev. Andrew Pataki, J.C.L., D.D., Bishop of Parma, Parma, Ohio
Rev. Z. Pazheparampil, S.J., Kenya, Africa
Simone Penner, Steinbach, Canada
Pat Rensing, Fountain Valley, California
Rose Rotondi, Boston, Massachusetts
Mary Ellen Santa, Huntington, Indiana
Jesse and Tish Sendejas, Houston, Texas
Rev. Kevin Shanley, O.Carm., Editor, *Carmelite Review*, Aylesford, Darien, Illinois
Gary Silva, Vacaville, California
Gjon Sinishta, Albanian Catholic Institute, San Francisco, California
Kathy Smith, Huntington, Indiana
Brother David Tejada, F.S.C., Santa Fe, New Mexico
JoAnn Thomas, Houston, Texas
Vennie Triana, Houston, Texas
Juliana Tubi, Adelphi, Maryland
Richard Valdez, Houston, Texas
Luis Vasquez, Houston, Texas
Bea Whitfil, Houston, Texas
Sister Gabrielle Woytko, Oxford, Michigan
Joannes Zheng, Beijing, People's Republic of China

Bibliography

Aguilar, Jeanette. *The Classic Cooking of Spain*. New York: Holt, Rinehart and Winston, 1966.

Ball, Ann. *A Litany of Saints*. Huntington, Ind.: Our Sunday Visitor Books, 1993.

Barolini, Helen. *Festa*. San Diego: Harcourt Brace Jovanovich, 1988.

Benedictine Sisters of Peking. *The Art of Chinese Cooking*. Tokyo: Charles Tuttle Co., 1956.

Boulting, E. Frances. *The Beautiful Childhood*, New York: Harcourt Brace and Co., 1926.

Brenuil. *Peruvian Dishes*. Lima: ABC, 1980.

Chalmers, Irena. *Great American Food Almanac*. New York: Harper and Row, 1986.

Dent, Huntley. *The Feast of Santa Fe*. New York: Simon and Schuster, 1985.

Elverson, Virginia, and McLanahan, Mary Ann. *A Cooking Legacy*. New York: Walker and Company, 1975.

Field, Michael and Frances. *A Quintet of Cuisines*. New York: Time-Life Books, 1970.

First Catholic Slovak Ladies Association. *The Anniversary Slovak-American Cook Book*. Chicago: Tylka Bros. Press, 1952.

Feibleman, Peter. *American Cooking: Creole and Acadian*. New York: Time-Life Books, 1971.

Friedlander, Barbara. *Vegetables, Fruits, and Nuts*. New York: Grosset and Dunlap, 1974.

Gaden, Eileen. *Biblical Garden Cookery*. Chappaqua, New York: Christian Herald Books, 1976.

Garza, Lucy. *South Texas Mexican Cook Book*. Austin, Tex.: Eakin Press, 1982.

Grieve, M. *A Modern Herbal*. New York: Dover Publications, 1982.

Harper, Rev. Howard V. *Days and Customs of All Faiths*. New York: Fleet Publishing, 1957.

Hazelton, Nika. *The Art of Scandinavian Cooking*. New York: The Macmillan Company, 1965.

————. *The Cooking of Germany*. New York: Time-Life Books, 1969.

Horsting, Maudie, and de Lannoy, Frona. *Flavors of Southeast Asia*. San Francisco: 101 Productions, 1979.

Hottes, Alfred Carl. *1001 Christmas Facts and Fancies*. New York: A.T. De La Mare Company, 1946.

James, E.O. *Christian Myth and Ritual, a Historical Study*. Gloucester, Mass.: Peter Smith, 1973.

Kaufman, William I., Ed. *The Catholic Cookbook*. New York: Citadel Press, 1965.

N/A, *Kolachki*. Johnston City, N.Y.: Ethnic Enterprises, 1984.

Lang, George. *Lang's Compendium of Culinary Nonsense and Trivia*. New York: Crown Publishers, 1980.

Linck, Ernestine, and Roach, Joyce. *Eats: A Folk History of Texas Foods*. Ft. Worth, Tex.: Texas Christian University Press, 1989.

McLoughlin, Helen. *Christmas to Candlemas*. Collegeville, Minn.: The Liturgical Press, 1956.

————. *Family Advent Customs*. Collegeville, Minn.: The Liturgical Press, 1956.

————. *Family Customs, Easter to Pentecost*. Collegeville, Minn.: The Liturgical Press, 1956.

————. *My Nameday, Come for Dessert*. Collegeville, Minn.: The Liturgical Press, 1962.

Moore, Elizabeth Butler, and Tavary, Cappie M., *La Festa di San Giuseppe*. Covington, La.: undated.

Nathan, Joan and Goldman, Judy. *The Flavor of Jerusalem*. Boston: Little, Brown and Company, 1975.

Ortiz, Elisabeth Lambert. *The Food of Spain and Portugal*. New York: Atheneum, 1989.

Our Lady of the Cedars Maronite Catholic Church. *Lebanese Cuisine*. Akron, Ohio: O.L. of the Cedars Church, 1985.

Polanie Club. *Treasured Polish Recipes for Americans*. Minneapolis: Polanie Publishing Company, 1988.

Poole, Shona Crawford. *The Christmas Cookbook*. New York: Atheneum, 1979.

Quintana, Patricia. *Mexico's Feasts of Life*. Tulsa: Council Oaks Books, 1989.

Rinzler, Carol Ann. *The Book of Chocolate*. New York: St. Martin's Press, 1977.

Rombauer, Irma S. *The Joy of Cooking*. Philadelphia: The Blakiston Company, 1943.

Schafer, Charles and Violet. *Breadcraft*. San Francisco: Yerba Buena Press, 1974.

St. George Ladies' Auxiliary. *A Collection of Treasured Hungarian Recipes*.

Courtland, Ontario: St. George Greek Catholic Church, 1976.

Sheraton, Mimi. *Visions of Sugarplums*. New York: Random House, 1968.

Steinberg, Rafael. *The Cooking of Japan*. New York: Time-Life Books, 1969.

The Editors of Time-Life Books. *The Holiday Cookbook*. New York: Time-Life Books, 1976.

Vaughn, Mary Ann Woloch. *Ukrainian Christmas*. Munster, Ind.: Ukrainian Heritage Company: 1983

Vaughn, Mary Ann Woloch. *Ukrainian Easter*. Munster, Ind.: Ukrainian Heritage Company: 1983.

Vehling, Joseph Dommers, Ed. Apicius. *Cookery and Dining in Imperial Rome*. New York: Dover Publications, 1977.

Vitz, Evelyn Birge. *A Continual Feast*. San Francisco: Ignatius Press, 1985.

Weiser, Francis X. *The Christmas Book*. New York: Harcourt, Brace and Company, 1952.

_____. *The Easter Book*. New York: Harcourt, Brace and Company, 1954.

_____. *Handbook of Christian Feasts and Customs*. New York: Harcourt, Brace and Company, 1952.

_____. *The Holyday Book*. New York: Harcourt, Brace and Company, 1956.

Indexes

A. Index of Types of Recipes

B. Ethnic Origins of Recipes

C. Alphabetical Listing of Recipes